The Cairngorms

published by
pocket mountains ltd
14 Belford Road, Edinburgh EH4 3BL
www.pocketmountains.com

ISBN: 0-9544217-2-8

Printed in Poland

Introduction

This guide features forty circular walks in the Cairngorms. It includes all of the Munros (peaks above 914m/3000ft) and many other hills that combine to make good circuits.

Routes have been chosen according to a number of factors, including variety of terrain, great views, historical interest, minimal road walking and the feasibility of a circular route.

Environmental factors such as the ability of access points to support additional cars and opportunities for bypassing visitor-sensitive or eroded areas have also been taken into account. Circular routes help to take the pressure off badly eroded paths, and walking in areas where there have been fewer footsteps is more conducive to natural regeneration of the land.

Walkers can also minimise their own impact on the environment by using purpose-built paths whenever possible and walking in single file to help prevent widening scars. Restricting your use of bikes to tracks, parking sensibly, avoiding fires and litter, and keeping dogs on a lead, particularly on grazing land and during lambing, all help to preserve the land and good relations with its inhabitants. Many of the responsibilities for walkers are now enshrined in law.

How to use this guide

The routes in this book are divided into five regions. These divisions largely represent points of access into the mountains, or use natural geographical boundaries. The opening section for each of the five regions introduces the area, its towns, topography and key features, and contains brief route outlines. It is supplemented by a road map, locating the walks.

Each route begins with an introduction identifying the names and heights of significant tops, the relevant Ordnance Survey (OS) map, total distance and average time. Many routes also contain an option for cycling part of the way where there is a long low-level approach.

A sketch map shows the main topographical details of the area and the route. The map is intended only to give the reader an idea of the terrain, and should not be followed for navigation.

Every route has an estimated round-trip time: this is for rough guidance only and should help in planning, especially when daylight hours are limited. In winter or after heavy rain, extra time should also be added for difficulties underfoot.

Risks and how to avoid them

Many of the hills in this guide are remote and craggy, and the weather in Scotland can change suddenly, reducing visibility to several yards. Winter walking brings particular challenges, including limited daylight, white-outs, cornices and avalanches. Every year, walkers and climbers die from falls or hypothermia in the Scottish mountains. Equally, though, overstretched Mountain Rescue teams are often called out to walkers who are simply tired or hungry.

Preparation for a walk should begin well before you set out, and your choice of route should reflect your fitness, the conditions underfoot and the regional weather forecasts.

None of the walks in this guide should be attempted without the relevant OS Map or equivalent at 1:50,000 (or 1:25,000) and a compass.

Even in summer, warm, waterproof clothing is advisable and footwear that is comfortable and supportive with good grips a must. Don't underestimate how much food and water you need and remember to take any medication required, including reserves in case of illness or delay. Many walkers also carry a whistle, first aid kit and survival bag.

It is a good idea to leave a route description with a friend or relative in case a genuine emergency arises: you should not rely on a mobile phone to get you out of difficulty. If walking as part of a group, make sure your companions are aware of any medical conditions, such as diabetes, and how to deal with problems that may occur.

There is a route for most levels of fitness in this guide, but it is important to know your limitations. Even for an experienced walker, colds, aches and pains can turn an easy walk into an ordeal.

These routes assume some knowledge of navigation in the hills with use of map and compass, though these skills are not difficult to learn. Use of Global Positioning System (GPS) devices is becoming more common but, while GPS can help pinpoint your location on the map in zero visibility, it cannot tell you where to go next.

Techniques such as scrambling or climbing on rock, snow and ice are required on just a few mountains in this guide. Such skills will improve confidence and the ease with which any route can be completed. They will also help you to avoid or escape potentially dangerous areas if you lose your way. The Mountaineering Council of Scotland provides training and information.

For most of these routes, proficiency in walking and map-reading is sufficient.

Access

Until the Land Reform (Scotland) Act was introduced early in 2003, the 'right to roam' in Scotland was a result of continued negotiations between government bodies, interest groups and landowners.

In many respects, the Act simply reinforces the common law right of access to the countryside of Scotland for recreational purposes. However, a key difference is that under the Act the right of access depends on whether it is exercised responsibly.

Landowners have a legal duty not to put up fences, walls or signs that prevent recreational users from crossing their land, but walkers should also take responsibility for their actions when exercising their right of access. Keep to paths and tracks where possible and, if in doubt, ask. At certain times of the year there are special restrictions, both at low level and on the hills, and these should be respected. Signs are usually posted at popular access points with details: there should be no expectation of a right of access to all places at all times.

The right of access does not extend to use of motor vehicles on private or estate roads.

Seasonal restrictions
Red and Sika deer stalking:
Stags: 1 July to 20 October
Hinds: 21 October to 15 February
Deer may also be culled at other times for welfare reasons. The seasons for Fallow and Roe deer (less common) are also longer. Many estates belong to the Hillphones network which provides advance notice of shoots.
Grouse shooting:
12 August to 10 December
Forestry:
Felling: all year
Planting: November to May
Heather burning:
September to April
Lambing:
March to May (Dogs should be kept on a lead at all times near livestock.)

Glossary
Common Gaelic words found in the text and maps:

abhainn	river
ailean	field; grassy plain
àirigh	summer hill pasture; shieling
allt	burn; stream
àth	ford
bàn	white
beag	small
bealach	pass; gap; gorge
beinn	ben; mountain
bràighe	neck; upper part
cìoch	breast; hub; pointed rock
clach	boulder; stone
cnoc	hillock
coire	corrie; cauldron; mountain hollow
creachann	exposed rocky summit
creag	cliff
cruach	heap; stack
dubh	black; dark
garbh	thick; coarse; rough
lagan	hollow; dimple
learg	hillside exposed to sea or sun
lochan	small loch; pool
meall	mound; lump; bunch
mór	big; great; tall
sgòrr	peak; cliff; sharp point
sgùrr	large conical hill
stùc	pinnacle; precipice; steep rock

This section includes the most southerly area of the Cairngorms, close to the cities of Perth and Dundee. The hills are generally lower than the rest of the Cairngorms but similar in character, with rounded moorland tops above dramatic and steep-sided valleys.

For more than 400 years, the fertile glens of this area were plundered by the cateran, freebooting cattle-raiding clansmen. Castles and outposts were often built to deter these costly raids, and eventually helped to bring stability.

This section contains two routes that start close to the Spittal of Glenshee and one by the notorious Devil's Elbow at the head of the glen. Five routes are spread across the famous Angus Glens: a gentle walk from Backwater Reservoir; two great mountain treks in Glen Clova; a circuit near the head

of the Water of Saughs; and a walk along the rivers of Lee and Mark at the end of Glen Esk.

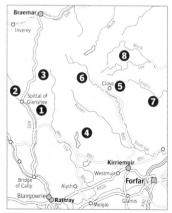

Glen Shee and the Braes o'Angus

Carn Ait and Diarmid's Tomb

Carn Ait (864m), **Black Hill** (757m)

Walk time 5h40 Height gain 700m
Distance 16km OS Map Landranger 43

A varied circuit across mountain, moor and farmland starting from the Spittal of Glenshee.

Start from the hotel at the Spittal of Glenshee (GR110699). (Park in the village.) Follow the loop road to the north side of the village where it joins the A93. Walk north along the main road to a stile on the right hand side after about 50m. Beyond the stile, a farm track leads east past a cottage to reach farm buildings at Tomb. Cross another stile (marked with a red heart) at the north end of Tomb to climb north by a track towards Bad an Lòin. Leave the track just short of a bealach after 1km, and bear eastwards over easy terrain to the summit of Carn an Daimh. Walk NNE, keeping to the higher ground, to reach the rocky top of Carn Ait (GR142732) (2h40). Drop down on the east side, and follow the fenceposts southeast over Mallrenheskein and up the boggy expanse of Black Hill (GR163718). Descend the southwest ridge towards Carn Dearg, and then drop south to join a good track. Follow this westwards for 3km towards Westerton of Runavey. At the junction with twin deer gates, take the track on the right to descend steeply to the farm buildings at Westerton. Immediately after the farm, the track trends south.

Instead of following this, go straight on over a stile and follow muddy tracks northwest to Tomb. Cross a stile at the top corner of the last field to avoid the buildings, and skirt around the north wall for 100m to reach the original stile. From here, it is a short walk back to the Spittal of Glenshee (5h40).

Diarmid's Tomb

According to legend, Diarmid was a warrior of great repute who fought and killed a demon boar near the Spittal of Glenshee. Unfortunately, he was wounded in the contest and the King threw away the potion that could save him as he knew Diarmid was having an affair with his Queen. At the foot of Bad an Lòin, a large mound was built over his grave in tribute.

◄ Full moon on Monamenach

Glas Tulaichean and Gleann Taitneach

Glas Tulaichean ⓜ (1051m)

Walk time 5h40 Height gain 700m
Distance 15km OS Map Landranger 43

A peak which affords great views over the hinterland of the southern Cairngorms. The initial climb from the glen is steep and crosses some rough terrain.

Start from Dalmunzie House, 3km northwest of the Spittal of Glenshee (GR091712). (Ask permission to park here, or leave vehicles 1.5km southeast at the estate entrance.) Take the road to Glenlochsie Farm and, from the farmyard, turn left through a waymarked gate. The track follows the river westwards, passing the remnants of a private railway. Leave the track where it fords the river, and climb

north to follow a fence and the old railway to a sturdy bridge. Cross the water, and climb steeply northwest over awkward heathery slopes soon after: these ease before arriving at the top of Creag Bhreac. Continue along the crest of the ridge until you reach an old grassy track after 1km. This winds northwest, taking you almost all of the way to the summit of Glas Tulaichean (GR051760) (3h20). Care is required on the summit as the cliffs around the corrie are steep. Follow a line of fenceposts northeastwards for about 500m to join the east ridge. After a short easy descent, a grassy track leads you into Glas Choire Mhór, doubling back west below a band of cliffs before dropping into the glen. Ford the river to meet a good gravel track on the east bank. Continue along the track for

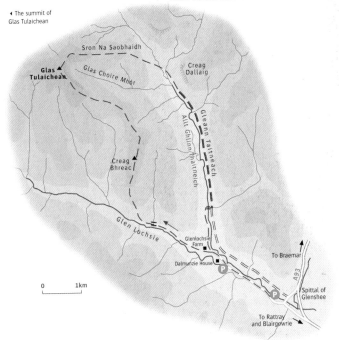

◄ The summit of Glas Tulaichean

about 5km to a bridge over a tributary and then a bridge over the Allt Ghlinn Thaitneich. After crossing the main river, follow a path to a fence. This takes you to a grassy track which leads first along the river and then continues south before reaching the road by a white gate just west of Dalmunzie House (5h40).

The Dalmunzie Railway

Built in the early 1920s by Sir Archibald Birkmyre to transport grouse shooting parties from Dalmunzie House (now a hotel) to the Glen Lochsie Shooting Lodge, the Dalmunzie Railway was a gloriously ostentatious piece of engineering. The two and a half miles of track, which gained 400 feet in height, were sold for scrap in the 1970s when all rail transport had to conform to British Rail regulations. The engine and carriages are in storage at the Dalmunzie House Hotel, and the path of the old rail track can still be seen.

11

Creag Leacach and Glas Maol

Glas Maol 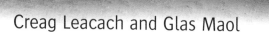 (1068m),
Creag Leacach (987m)

Walk time 4h20 Height gain 700m
Distance 10km OS Map Landranger 43

**A short walk which starts high in Glen
Shee to give views of The Cairnwell
and the higher peaks of the Cairngorms.
There is a small river crossing on return.**

Start from the large parking area on the
east side of the A93, 2.5km south of the
Glenshee Ski Centre (GR138757). Drop
south down the embankment, and use the
stepping stones to cross the burn. From
here, a good path climbs steeply eastwards

to gain the ridge of Leacann Dubh: this
leads more gently northwards. Ignore the
track for the ski centre after 2km, and bear
east to ascend the knoll of Meall Odhar. A
path continues eastwards, climbing steeply
to reach the plateau of Glas Maol and its
summit (GR167766) (2h40). From the trig
point, walk southwest over gentle terrain
for 1km and then south along the main
ridge to a bealach. A rollercoaster of a wall
leads SSW to the summit of Creag Leacach
(GR154745) (3h40). Follow the ridge
southwest for 800m to a smaller top, and
then descend northwest to the bealach
before Meall Gorm. Instead of ascending

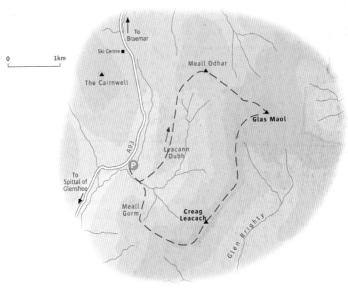

◄ Carn Bhinnein and Creag Leacach
from Glas Tulaichean

this knoll, drop directly north into a small heathery glen. Ford the burn where convenient, and continue downstream through the canyon. This emerges close to the original path, which takes you back to your start point (4h20).

The Cateran

Cateran derives from the Gaelic word *ceathairne*, meaning 'peasantry', but came to be applied to the fighting men of Highland clans. Glen Shee was a good cattle-raising area and between the 13th and 17th centuries was frequently raided by bands of cateran, usually 50- to 100-men strong, from various northern clans. Locals who were subjected to a raid often paid dearly. One infamous attack around the Spittal of Glenshee is said to have left twenty widows in each of the three villages targeted. The advent of firearms put a stop to large-scale cattle raids and so brought a bloody era in Highland history to an end.

Backwater Reservoir

Corwharn (611m)

Walk time 5h Height gain 400m
Distance 16km OS Map Landranger 44

**A varied and intricate route starting
from the flooded glen and leading
across farmland, through a gorge and
over moor.**

Start at the large parking bay and picnic
benches towards the north end of Backwater
Reservoir (GR257615). Walk south along the
road for 200m to the end of a plantation
where there is a gate on the left. Pass
through, and climb southeast by the side of
the forest to a second gate. Keeping above
the ruined farm of Ley, cut ESE over the field

to a fence with two gates about 150m east
of the ruins. The gate on the left leads to a
grassy track which is easily followed
through the glen. Higher up, a rocky path
leads down the narrow gorge beneath Craig
of Balloch. It rises slightly, and passes
through a gate and a field to reach the road
in Glen Quharity by some straggly pine.
Follow the road north to Longdrum, and
then continue northeast along a track. After
800m, this branches: take the left fork to
climb northwest beside the field and a strip
of forest. This turns into a good track which
bears north up the ridge of Milldewan Hill:
further up, it contours around the top and
joins a fence. Follow this northeast along

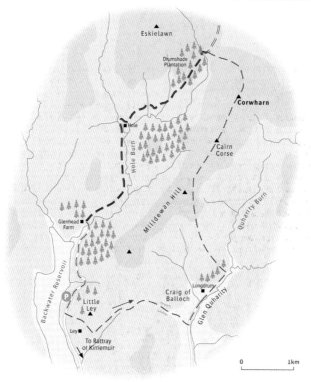

the ridge, over Cairn Corse and to the top of Corwharn with its neatly stacked cairn (GR288651) (3h). Cross the stile on the summit where the two fences converge, and follow the new fence northeast by peat hags before shortly descending northwest to a bealach. Walk west for 50m to find a track which crosses the Hole Burn, and then rises to the top of Drumshade Plantation. After a gate, the track slips between forests of differing age. Once you have left the plantation, follow the track westwards through several gates to Hole, then south to a junction at Glenhead Farm. The road leads south back to the start point (5h).

◀ Mount Blair above Glen Isla, west of the reservoir

Corries of Glen Doll

Mayar ⓜ (928m), **Driesh ⓜ** (947m)

Walk time 5h20 Height gain 900m
Distance 13km OS Map Landranger 44

An adventurous walk through the spectacular Corrie Fee with an exposed descent along The Scorrie, the steep north ridge of Driesh.

Start from the Forestry Commission car park at the end of the public road in Glen Clova (GR283761). Walk westwards along the road towards Acharn, turning left after 200m to follow footpath signs. The road leads past farm buildings, and turns to track at a gate and stile. Carry straight on along Jock's Road at the intersection beyond. After 1km, leave this to follow the main track to the river. Cross by a bridge and climb southwest, ignoring a track on the right. The main track diminishes to a path, and leaves the forest by a stile to reveal the vast amphitheatre of Corrie Fee. Follow a path over flat ground towards the back of the corrie. A path to the left of two sets of waterfalls makes a careful zigzag ascent, avoiding steeper ground. Above the falls, keep close to the burn and ascend easier ground towards the plateau before climbing southeast to the summit of Mayar (GR241738) (3h). From the top, follow the wide east flank to meet the path signposted for Kilbo after about 1km. Continue eastwards between two fences. After 800m, the old fence on the right ends and the new one on the left turns north. [Escape: about 40m northeast of the last of the old posts, there is a large cairn. The Kilbo path descends along the Shank of Drumfollow and back to Acharn.] Drop southeast to a shallow bealach, and follow a path steeply to the plateau of Driesh. Continue east to the summit and trig point

◄ Ben Reid, Hill of Strone and Driesh

(GR271736) (4h). Descend NNE over gentle ground for 1km to reach the sharp ridge of The Scorrie. A narrow path navigates the lip of Winter Corrie (care is required around the steep cliffs), before weaving down The Scorrie on or just to the left of the apex: any steep or exposed sections are short-lived. At the corner of a plantation, follow the fence towards Glen Clova. About 150m before the flats, watch for a trapdoor in the fence, marked Scorrie Path, which beckons you into the forest. This soon leads to a stile with a track beyond. Turn left onto the track, which doubles back to cross the White Water. Join Jock's Road to return to the start (5h20).

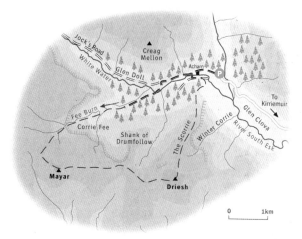

Jock's Road

When wealthy Duncan Macpherson returned from his stay in Australia in the late 19th century to buy the Glen Doll Estate, he immediately put a ban on people walking across his land. Many objected and one, Jock Winter, defied the ruling, which led to the Scottish Rights of Way and Recreation Society setting up signs on the estate. After a long court battle which went all of the way to the House of Lords, Macpherson eventually lost his case in 1888, leaving both he and the Rights Society bankrupt.

Brandy and Wharral

Green Hill (870m),
Ben Tirran (The Goet) Ⓒ (896m)

Walk time 5h20 Height gain 900m
Distance 14km OS Map Landranger 44

A steep climb to reach a wide plateau, passing a picturesque corrie loch on approach and another on return.

Start at the Glen Clova Hotel (GR327731). (Public parking 100m to the west over the humpback bridge.) Walk north through the hotel car park and past a triple-roofed building to a schoolhouse. Follow the path signposted for Glen Esk until you reach a burn above the plantation. Take a smaller path that climbs by fenceposts along the west bank, and eases just before the picturesque Loch Brandy. From here, climb steeply north along the prominent ridge of The Snub to a cairn. Contour northwards around the corrie rim, taking care to avoid the cliffs. A path leads east to the cairn at the top of Green Hill. Continue eastwards through occasional bog, keeping to the undulating higher ground. At White Hill, bear southeast to climb the final slopes to the trig point of The Goet, the summit of Ben Tirran (GR373746) (3h40). Descend gently southwest and then steeply west to the end of Loch Wharral. Contour and then drop southwest towards Rough Craig. Before reaching this knoll, descend west towards a

burn and cross it by an old fence. A new fence hugs the west bank: follow this over rough ground on the right hand side, and then continue your descent on an old zigzagging track. When it reaches a plantation, the track leads 200m west to a gateway where a narrow path takes you on through sparse birch to a lochan. Various sheep tracks lead to the road. Walk the last 1.5km along the tarmac to the hotel (5h20).

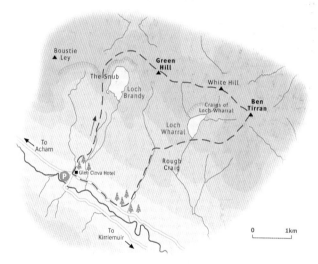

Kirriemuir's lost boys

This small town's most celebrated son is James Matthew Barrie (1860-1937), author of the children's play, *Peter Pan*, the tale of the boy who would not grow up. His boyhood home, now maintained by the National Trust for Scotland, can be visited at 9 Brechin Road and he is buried in the town cemetery. Also born in Kirriemuir was Bon Scott (1946-1980), the charismatic lead singer with Australian rockers AC/DC. Before his untimely death in London at the height of his fame, he enjoyed worldwide success with classics such as 'Highway to Hell' and 'Whole Lotta Rosie'.

◄ Summit of Ben Tirran (The Goet)

The Water of Saughs

Ruragh (735m), **Hill of Glansie** (726m)

Walk time 4h40 Height gain 600m
Distance 13km OS Map Landranger 44

**A short but interesting route in the
rolling hills north of the prehistoric
Caterthuns.**

Start from the end of the public road at a
parking area close to the entrance of
Waterhead Farm (GR464716). Follow the
track northwest along the Water of Saughs
to reach a suspension bridge after 1.5km. In
high winds, the crossing provides some
excitement. Beyond, climb eastwards
towards Corrie na Berran. Do not enter the
corrie, but continue steeply northwards to
gain the ridgeline. Bear more easily
southwest over the top of the hill and down
to a bealach with a grassy track. Just to the
south of the bealach, there is a steading
and a junction. [Escape: climb gently
eastwards, and on over Hill of Berran to
Waterhead Farm.] Two tracks lead
southwestwards: take the upper of these to
follow the ridge by a fence to the rounded
summit of Ruragh. Descend southwest to a
boggy bealach, and climb Dog Hillock.
Rejoin the fenceposts here: these lead
eastwards to a track which takes you
along the ridge to the trig point of Hill of

Glansie (GR430698) (3h20). Descend ESE along the rough track until the terrain flattens out after about 1km. Follow the fencing eastwards over Birse Shades and Mount Shed, and down to a bealach shared with Hill of Mondurran. Here a stile crosses the fence, but the old path (indicated on OS maps) is now almost non-existent. What remains of it bears northeast to Waterhead, losing height steadily and crossing a fence by a gate to reach a wooden bridge south of the farm. Climb to and pass between the farm buildings to reach the start point (4h40).

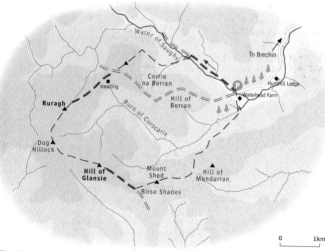

The Caterthuns

The Brown and White Caterthuns, two forts on neighbouring hills, are located south of the Water of Saughs between Brechin and Glen Lethnot. The forts have been dated to around 500BC, and there is evidence of several periods of building and occupation. With its two wide circles of stones, the White Caterthun is one of the best prehistoric sites in the country. The Brown Caterthun is more extensive, with up to six lines of defence, but more difficult to appreciate as the heather has encroached.

◀ Burn of Corscarie near Waterhead

The Wolf and the Cateran

Wolf Craig (715m)

Walk time 5h40 Height gain 500m
Distance 17km OS Map Landranger 44

A walk along the dramatic, narrow glens of Mark and Lee, passing several great waterfalls. This route is ideal for water lovers and involves an optional river crossing.

Start at the car park at the end of the public road in Glen Esk (GR446804). Walk west along the road for 200m, and then turn right onto a track towards the House of Mark. Just before the house, turn left onto a grassy track with a gate. This continues northwest as a good rocky path to a bridge.

[Variant: to avoid fording the river further on, cross to the south bank here.] Rather than go over the bridge, follow the track past the Queen's Well to cross after 1km. (A reasonable path continues on the north side, but there are no easy stepping stones for at least 4km after this point.) Continue on the south bank past waterfalls: just east of Balnamoon's Cave, the river has worn the rock into fantastic shapes. About 1km beyond the cave and the higher falls, a small burn flows eastwards from the summit of Wolf Craig. Follow the burn through a channel scarred by the debris of natural erosion to reach the final heathery slopes and five cairns which

mark the top of Wolf Craig (GR380824) (3h40). Descend east for 300m, and then follow the vague southeast ridge towards a plantation. Drop down on the west side of the trees to reach a track along the scenic Glen Lee. Follow the track eastwards past Loch Lee and Invermark Castle to the start point (5h40).

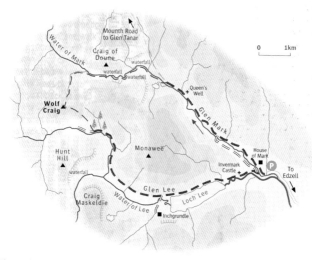

The Kitchen of Angus

The Lindsay lairds of Edzell and Glenesk, who built the present Edzell Castle and lived on the site for 360 years, were renowned for their opulent lifestyle. When they had finished with their lavish meals, the poor of the area would gather in the courtyard to feed from the excellent scraps. As a result, Edzell Castle became known as the Kitchen of Angus. The wealth of Glen Esk also attracted Caterans from the north who would sporadically raid the fertile glens. Invermark Castle was built in the 16th century as a strategic outpost as it looked out to the Mounth road which linked Aberdeenshire with Angus. The raiders still cost Edzell Castle dearly and, in 1647, David Lindsay claimed losses of almost £100,000, although his extravagant lifestyle probably accounted for much of that figure.

◀ Loch Lee from Inchgrundle

This region contains many rounded hills, some great sweeping ridges and few crags. Further north towards Dalwhinnie, the high moorland is more typical of the central Cairngorms. All of these routes are easily accessible from the A9 or the Highland Line between Perth and Inverness.

Transport links to the north of Scotland did not always provide such an easy or direct journey. The Jacobite rebellions of 1715 and 1745 highlighted the difficulty with which government troops moved around the country, and so began a long campaign of mapping and military road building. This included a road through the Drumochter Pass to link Blair Atholl with Inverness, which replaced the high-level Minigaig as the new route to the north.

Half of the routes in this section involve long approaches, so use of a bike is recommended for access. Three routes start from Glen Tilt: two follow the glen to climb distant peaks; and one heads north along the Minigaig. There are two circuits on

Beinn a'Ghlo: one leaves from the high road between Pitlochry and Glen Shee; the other starts near Blair Atholl. One short walk begins from the battle site of Killiecrankie. Walks along the Gaick over the Drumochter Pass and through Glen Truim from Dalwhinnie complete the set.

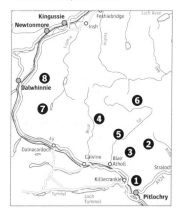

Pitlochry to Dalwhinnie

Ben Vrackie from the Soldier's Leap

Ben Vrackie ⓒ (841m)

Walk time 4h40 Height gain 700m
Distance 12km OS Map Landranger 43

Ben Vrackie is a popular peak close to Pitlochry. This walk follows good tracks and paths to make a half-day circuit.

Start from the National Trust for Scotland Visitor Centre on the B8019, at the east end of Killiecrankie (GR917627). Walk north to the bridge and cross the road. Follow the sign for Old Faskally Chalets: a single-track road passes under the A9 and winds up to a collection of buildings. From here, follow the road east to the Boy's Brigade bench and then south up to the water treatment works and an intersection. Bear northeast by a rising grassy track, passing through two gates. After 500m, the track splits at a path marker: the right turning takes you to a stile over a high wall. Beyond, the track rises southeastwards for 2km until just under Meall na h-Aodainn Móire. A path on the left, signposted for Loch a'Choire, takes you around the hill and down to the loch below Ben Vrackie. Walk around the east side of the water, and climb NNE by the steep renovated path to the summit of Ben Vrackie (GR950632) (3h). Walk 200m northeast to a small knoll before descending WNW along a good ridge: a path winds its way over the crest to the boulder crown of Meall an Daimh. Head for the west side of the peak where two walls

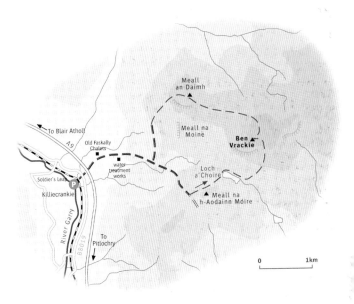

meet: one accompanies a fence north, the other descends WSW. Follow the latter by a poor path on the left, dropping in fits and starts for 500m to reach a track by a low crag. Walk southeast along this track before descending to join the original grassy track which leads back to Killiecrankie (4h40).

Killiecrankie and the Soldier's Leap

The celebrated battle of 1689 between the government forces of William of Orange, led by General Hugh Mackay, and the Jacobite forces under 'Bonnie Dundee', Graham of Claverhouse, saw the loss of nearly 3000 men and resulted in a hollow victory for the Highlanders as Bonnie Dundee perished in battle. Towards the north end of the Pass of Killiecrankie is the famous Soldier's Leap, where one of Mackay's men jumped the chasm to escape his pursuers. Today the oak and mixed deciduous woodland is preserved by the National Trust for Scotland which acquired the site in 1947.

◀ Ben Vrackie from Meall na h-Aodainn Móire

Beinn a'Ghlo

Beinn a'Ghlo: Carn nan Gabhar ⓜ(1129m)

Walk time 5h40 Height gain 900m
Approach and return 2h20 bike or 5h walk
Distance 15km + 20km approach and return
OS Map Landranger 43

**A remote peak with a high ridge
which is best approached by bike.
Beinn a'Ghlo is the highest mountain in
the area and provides great views.**

Start 500m east of the hamlet of
Straloch on the A924, just east of a bridge
by the private road signposted for
Glenfernate/Fealar (GR051638). (Park on
the west side of the bridge.) Cycle or walk
north up the road to a fork after about 1km,
and turn right to pass the farm buildings of
Glenfernate Lodge. Continue north, gaining
gradual height by the Allt Fearnach (the No
Entry sign on the tree does not apply to
walkers or cyclists), crossing the river
towards Daldhu after 6km. Take a grass
track on the left 200m before the house:
this leads to a gravel track which rises and
falls alongside the Allt Glen Loch. Before
the track reaches the bottom of the glen
after a further 3km, it meets another track
(GR997718). Bikes are best left here:
walk times start from this point. Continue
west to ford a river by the remains of a

shieling: the track climbs for a while before levelling out near the rounded bealach south of Meall na h-Eilrig. Descend to the bealach, and then contour west under the slopes of Airgiod Bheinn. Rather than make a complete traverse of the peak, choose a suitable point to begin your ascent. The slopes are quite steep and alternate between scree and grass, but it is not difficult to reach the main ridge. Follow the rocky crest of the ridge to the top of Airgiod Bheinn. Continue northwards, descending gently, and keep to the ridge as it curves northeast. A further 1km of gentle ascent

leads to the summit and trig point of Carn nan Gabhar (GR971732) (3h20). Descend NNE along the ridge, carefully avoiding the cliffs of Coire Cas-eagallach, and then continue northwards along the ridge to climb a small knoll and Meall a'Mhuirich. Continue north and, at the bealach before Meall Gharran, descend slopes on the east to the foot of the hourglass Loch Loch. A path on the east shore takes you southwards, turning to a grassy track just beyond the head of the loch: this leads back to the original track (5h40). Return along Gleann Fearnach to the start.

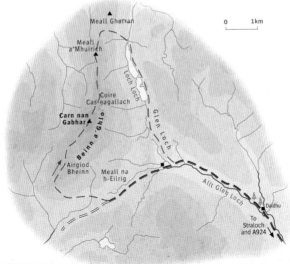

◄ Beinn a'Ghlo from Glen Tilt

The ridge over Glen Tilt

Carn Liath Ⓜ (975m), **Bràigh Coire Chruinn-bhalgain** Ⓜ (1070m)

Walk time 7h Height gain 1000m
Distance 18km OS Map Landranger 43

An ascent of two peaks on the Beinn a'Ghlo massif. The route starts high and follows stalkers' paths over rough ground.

Start by a cattle grid at the end of the public road to Monzie, by Loch Moraig (GR906672). (Park on the verge either side of the cattle grid.) Walk 200m east along the road to a gate for Shinagag Farm, and follow the track beyond to reach a pair of steadings after 2km: these mark the start of the usual ascent path to Carn Liath, now heavily eroded. Ignore this route and, instead, continue east

along the track for a further 2km to a flattened area of gravel on your right. (This is about 150m before a fork in the track.) At the end of the gravel, a stalkers' path trends northeast to pass immediately over a twin knoll. Follow this path over heather and bog for about 1.5km to a burn before Beinn Bheag, and then follow the burn upstream through more heather and tussocky grass. Higher up, where the burn widens and the corrie starts to open up, leave the ravine and climb steeply southwest to gain the summit of Carn Liath (GR935698) (3h20). Descend by the north ridge, which is steep-sided in places but never too narrow, as it swings northeast and then drops suddenly north to a bealach. Climb steeply east along the same path and then due north to the summit of Bràigh Coire Chruinn-bhalgain

◄ Carn Liath from the road to Monzie

(GR945724) (4h40). Descend the southwest ridge: this is gentle at first, but steepens towards a burn which is followed to flatter ground. Keeping the height, take to the heather in a southwesterly direction: if you can find the stalkers' path it will make for easier walking to the ruins of Creag-choinnich Lodge. Follow a good track back to the farm at Monzie. From here, it is just a short walk to the start (7h).

The Atholl Highlanders

Queen Victoria presented the Duke of Atholl's Highland bodyguard, the Atholl Highlanders, with their colours in 1845 while visiting Dunkeld, thus making them the only private army in Britain, a status they still enjoy today. At their greatest strength the Atholl Highlanders mustered four companies, each with 40 men, and for a time the officers appeared on the Army List. A revival in 1966 brought the number back up to around 50, and membership is a much-sought after honour in the region.

Over the Minigaig to Beinn Dearg

Beinn a'Chait (899m),
Beinn Dearg ⓜ (1008m)

Walk time 6h40 Height gain 1000m
Approach and return 2h bike or 4h40 walk
Distance 19km + 15km approach and return
OS Map Landranger 43

**A full day out on an historic route
over remote moorland. A mountain
bike will improve access and provide an
exciting return.**

Start from the Atholl Estate car park in
Old Bridge of Tilt, 1km north of Blair Atholl
(GR874663). Turn left onto the road and
walk or cycle west for 500m, then turn right
to reach Old Blair. Go straight on at the
crossroads and enter woodland: follow the
north bank of Banvie Burn along an
excellent track, pass through a gate and
continue northwards across the open fell.
At a prominent cairn, the track fords the
river and continues to gain height. Later, it
crosses the Allt an t-Seapail at a wooden
bridge (GR844722). Leave mountain bikes
here: walk times begin at this point. Follow
the burn northwards between Meall Tionail
and Carn Dearg Mór. Where the burn
disappears, cross a track and ascend the
broad western slopes of Beinn a'Chait to
the summit (GR865748) (2h). Bear NNW
over the plateau, avoiding the steep eastern
flanks overlooking Gleann Diridh, before

dropping to a boggy bealach shared with Beinn Dearg. Climb the south ridge, either by a path on the left or right of the apex, to the summit of Beinn Dearg (GR853778) (3h20). Descend on the north side, keeping to the high ground, and continue over one small mound. About 1km after the summit, drop west into bog to the north of the Allt Beinn Losgarnaich. Walk south along the west bank of this burn by a path. This makes a dramatic descent at the edge of the steep ravine and its hidden waterfalls before zigzagging to the floor of the glen. Join the track to Bruar Lodge here. At the lodge, bear west as if to cross the bridge and find the path that runs south between the river and a fence. Where the fence ends, the path climbs diagonally across the hillside (this may be hard to find when the heather is high) before dropping to join a track. Climb south over the bealach and return to the wooden bridge (6h40). Walk or cycle along the track to the start.

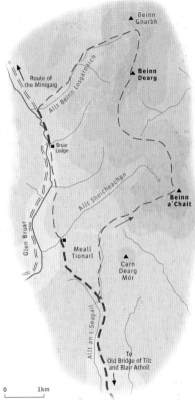

The drover's choice

The Minigaig was the main drove road from Blair Atholl to Kingussie until military engineers completed the road over the Drumochter Pass in the 18th century. Despite the new road, drovers continued to use the Minigaig because it was toll-free, had a soft surface for the beasts and good grazing en route. It is the highest north-south route in the Highlands, reaching an elevation of 836m.

◀ Glen Tilt from Carn Bhac

The Waterfall of Balaneasie

Bràigh nan Creagan Breac (887m),
Carn a'Chlamain ⓜ(963m)

Walk time 4h40 Height gain 800m
Approach and return 1h40 bike or 4h walk
Distance 12km + 16km approach and return
OS Map Landranger 43

**A simple horseshoe which starts at the
heart of Glen Tilt. Use of a bike will
speed access along the glen.**

Start from the Atholl Estate car park in
Old Bridge of Tilt (GR874663), 1km north of
Blair Atholl. There are several options for
access along the glen: the most direct,
described here, is suitable for both walkers
and cyclists. Take the track (marked Private

Road) from the right hand side of the house
opposite the car park. This climbs north,
steeply at first, and then follows the River
Tilt through woods, crossing the water after
2km. Continue upstream for a further 4km,
passing Marble Lodge and its humpback
bridge. There is another small bridge,
erected by army engineers, about 800m
beyond (GR909720). Bikes should be left
here: walk times are given from this point.
Climb steeply along the west bank of the
Allt Craoinidh until the waterfall comes into
view. Continue northwards up heather-
covered slopes until the ridge becomes
more defined at Sròn a'Chrò: here, an old
wall can be followed for some distance to

◄ The slopes of Beinn a'Ghlo from Glen Tilt, east of Carn a'Chlamain

its end. Keep the high ground as much as possible, bearing north over Bràigh Clais Daimh, Bràigh nan Creagan Breac and Aonach na Cloiche Móire. Then turn and bear southeast, climbing gently to the scree-laden summit of Carn a'Chlamain (GR915758) (3h20). Descend southeast, following a track along the broad ridge. After 1km, veer SSW along the pronounced ridge of Fàire Clach-ghlais. This becomes more defined further down where it is scored by a wide gravel track. Closer to the glen, when it switches to the east, leave the track to descend a steep path southwards to the bridge (4h40). Return to Old Bridge of Tilt.

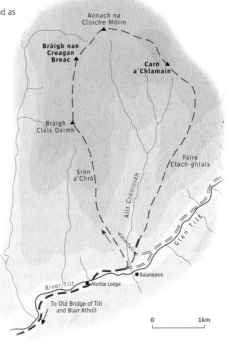

Aonach na
Cloiche Móire

Bràigh nan
Creagan
Breac

Carn
a'Chlamain

Bràigh
Clais Daimh

Fàire
Clach-ghlais

Sròn
a'Chrò

Allt Craoinidh

Waterfall

Glen Tilt

River Tilt ■ Balaneasie
■ Marble Lodge

To Old Bridge of Tilt
and Blair Atholl

0   1km

The War with the Duke

The current access rights are a result of 150 years of negotiation with landowners. The Association for the Protection of Public Rights of Roadway started in 1845 to promote access rights and, in particular, the protection of tracks over the mountains which linked inhabited glens. Two years after its foundation a landmark case came to court, known as the War with the Duke, when a party of students who wanted to walk up Glen Tilt were chased off the Atholl estate. The Court of Session later ruled against the Duke of Atholl.

Sgarsoch from Glen Tilt

An Sgarsoch ⓜ (1006m),
Carn an Fhidhleir ⓜ (994m)

Walk time 6h40 + detour 40 min
Height gain 800m
Approach and return 3h40 bike
Distance 20km + 32km approach and return
OS Map Landranger 43

A strenuous circuit in very remote country. The long approach is best made by mountain bike. A river crossing on return is optional, but bypassing it will add time to your journey.

Start from the Atholl Estate car park in Old Bridge of Tilt (GR874663). Take the track (marked Private Road) from the right hand side of the house opposite the car park. This runs the length of Glen Tilt, crossing and recrossing the river higher up. Follow the track past a forest lodge and to a junction 3km beyond the end of a narrow forest: here, the track leaves the River Tilt to climb northwards while a path continues along the glen (GR971775). Leave bikes here: walk times start from this point. Take the path by the river. After 2.5km, this meets the Tarf Water where the Bedford memorial bridge crosses the falls. Leave the Tilt 100m after the bridge to climb vague switchbacks northwards to flatter, boggier terrain. Continue northwards up the increasingly pronounced ridge of Sron Coire na Creige. The ground around Coire na Creige is littered with cairns, relics of a time when this area was much more popular. Follow the ridge and the county boundary west over unusually firm ground to Bràigh Coire Caochan nan Laogh. Descend northwest, and climb to Carn Greannach. From here, follow the long

◀ Leachdann Féith Seasgachain and the Tarf Water

westward sweeping arc around An Glas Choire to the flat summit of An Sgarsoch (GR933837) (3h40). Descend the southwest ridge to a bealach, and then climb grassy slopes westwards to join the south ridge of Carn an Fhidhleir. [Detour: walk NNW to reach the summit, and return along the same ridge (add 40 min).] Keep the high ground, and descend south to Leachdann Féith Seasgachain before dropping into the wide glen of the Allt a'Chaorainn

towards the Tarf Water. Follow this east for 2.5km to the remains of a bridge and a barn on the opposite bank. Ford the river here to reach a good track, which is easily followed across the bealach under Dùn Mór and down to the River Tilt (6h40). [Variant: if the Tarf cannot be crossed, continue along the north bank to the Bedford Bridge, and then follow the Tilt downstream (add 40 min).] Return through Glen Tilt to the start.

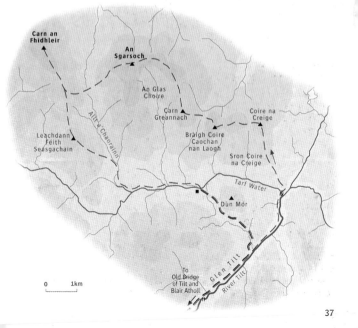

The Infamous Gaick

Glas Mheall Mór (928m), **A'Bhuidheanach Bheag** Ⓜ (936m), **Carn na Caim** Ⓜ (941m)

Walk time 5h40 Height gain 700m
Approach and return 1h40 bike or 4h walk
Distance 18km + 18km approach and return
OS Map Landranger 42

A high and lonely traverse over moorland from a mountain pass with a dark history. This route is best accessed by mountain bike.

Start from the snow gates on the A9 by Dalnacardoch Lodge (GR722702). (Park on the minor road with care.) A track on the north side of the road climbs steadily north through forest and above the Edendon Water before crossing the river, by bridge and then a ford, to reach Sronphadruig

Lodge. A small bridge is located 600m beyond the lodge (GR716789). Leave bikes here: walk times begin from this point. Cross the bridge, and bear due west over boggy moorland. The ground steepens as it approaches the top of Am Meadar. Follow the ridgeline southwest, and then over gently rising terrain to the rounded hump of Glas Mheall Mór with its small cairn. Drop to the northeast, and climb easily westwards to the summit of A'Bhuidheanach Bheag (GR660775) (2h40). Head northwards, following fenceposts for a short distance until they trend east, and then descend slightly before climbing A'Bhuidheanach. A track winds northeast over the highest ground for about 3km and, when it disappears, fencing leads to the rounded

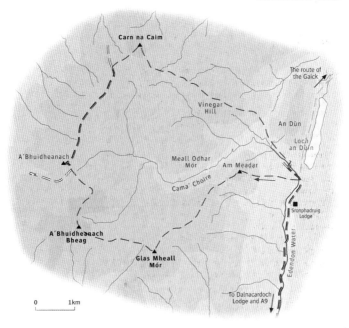

summit of Carn na Caim (GR677822). Bear ESE over peat bog, aiming for the whaleback shape of An Dùn, a much less imposing peak from this side. After Vinegar Hill, the terrain steepens for a short while before dropping into Cama' Choire. Follow the river to a weir: from here, a track leads back to the bridge near Sronphadruig Lodge (5h40). Return to Dalnacardoch.

The Gaick

The winding pass of the Gaick is prone to avalanche and has been associated with many bleak tales. In 1800 the lives of five soldiers, including the Black Officer John MacPherson, an unpopular recruiting captain, were lost here. MacPherson lived at Balachroan between Kingussie and Newtonmore, and was thought by locals to be in cahoots with the Devil. Their suspicions were founded on the abundance of the captain's crops and the fact that he used stone from the former parish church to refurbish his home.

◄ Sunrise at Dalnamein, east of Dalnacardoch

Meall Chuaich from Glen Truim

Meall Chuaich ⓜ (951m),
A'Mharconaich (882m)

Walk time 7h Height gain 900m
Distance 20km OS Map Landranger 42

**A circuit of two rounded peaks with
an intricate start but good access
tracks.**

Start at a gate to Cuaich from the old
military road, 3km northeast of Dalwhinnie
(GR653876). (Park 400m south.) Go through
the gate, over the River Truim, across the
railway line and into Cuaich. At the
crossroads by the houses, turn left to pass
through a corrugated tunnel under the A9.
Turn right to walk southwards (parallel to
the main road), and take the track on the
left which leads to another track beside the
aqueduct. Follow this east past a power
station and over a bridge to an intersection:
take the track on the left which leads up
the glen. Ignore two left turnings for Loch
Cuaich, and continue past a wooden shed
and across the Allt Coire Chuaich. About
70m after this bridge, a path on the left
starts to climb steeply northeast over
occasionally boggy ground. Where the
terrain becomes rockier, the path trends
east to climb several false tops before
reaching the summit of Meall Chuaich
(GR717878) (3h20). Drop SSE over
heathery slopes to a bealach above
Coire Chuaich. [Escape: join the track
which leads westwards back to the start.]
An old path, clearly visible from Meall
Chuaich, climbs southwards in zigzags from

the bealach. Further up, where it reaches a wide groove made by a burn, the path becomes more difficult to follow. Climb to the top of the plateau, and walk WSW over boggy and folded ground towards the summit of A'Mharconaich, which is marked only by an angled fencepost in a circular rock (GR708848). Descend southwest, aiming for Creag Liath. A track cuts down the east side of this knoll and leads northwards, turning to gravel before it reaches the original track along the Allt Cuaich. Retrace your steps to the start (7h).

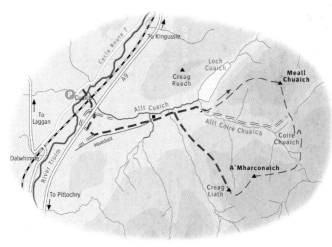

Sustrans and the National Cycle Network

The National Cycle Network is a system of cycleways and paths across Britain, and has been run by the charity Sustrans since 1995. The network uses minor roads, towpaths, old railway lines and newly built tracks, with routes in the countryside as well as in cities. It is estimated that by 2010 the network will comprise 15,000 miles across Britain. Route 7 is the Lochs and Glens route, which runs from Carlisle to Inverness. It uses the old military roads alongside the A9 for much of the way. Most of these are attributed to General Wade, although it was his successor Caulfeild who finished the link to Inverness and filled in the gaps.

Aviemore is the gateway to Scotland's second national park and, with easy access to the ski slopes and excellent walking country, it has long been the focal point for sports and tourism in the Cairngorms.

The town is geared towards a whole range of mountain activities including skiing and snowboarding, biking, boating, summer and winter climbing, and walking. There are numerous shops, rental outlets and other services catering for ski and outdoor enthusiasts, and year-round entertainment in the form of lively clubs, pubs, restaurants and cafés.

Aviemore provides the quickest access to the Cairngorm plateau, whose rounded tops and deep corries present a striking contrast to the low rolling hills and moorland that make up the rest of Speyside.

This section includes two routes that begin from the forests of Glen Feshie, three

challenging circuits on Cairn Gorm, Braeriach and Bynack More, and one easier walk beginning in Glen More. A further two walks start east of Grantown-on-Spey.

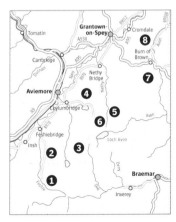

Aviemore and Speyside

Forests of Glen Feshie

Carn Bàn Mór (1052m),
Mullach Clach à Bhlàir ⓜ (1019m)

Walk time 7h40 Height gain 800m
Distance 22km OS Map Landranger 43

A traverse over the rounded hills above Glen Feshie and a long stroll through delightful Caledonian forest.

Start from the car park about 600m north of Auchlean near the end of the public road from Feshiebridge (GR852982). Walk south along the road until you spot the roof of the farmhouse, then take a good path east towards woodland. After crossing a stile, follow the upper path through the plantation. Exit at another stile, and climb slowly east along the path. This leads after 3km to a high point on the broad ridge of Carn Bàn Mór. The summit is just a short detour north from the main path. Return to the path to descend gradually to the southeast before climbing gently to Mòine Mhór. Follow the stony track that snakes southwestwards over the hills for 3km. When it turns southeast under Mullach Clach à Bhlàir, leave the track to climb to the summit of this peak (GR883927) (4h40). Descend southwest to join a prominent rounded ridge marked with occasional cairns and rock shelters. This is followed WSW to a lochan and new cairn beyond. Maintain the same bearing down steep slopes, watching for a well-hidden path which zigzags northwest through the heather. It crosses a small burn above the treeline before descending into the old forest where it continues northwards for 1km, losing altitude slowly. The path

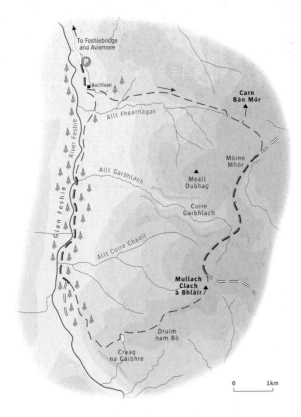

then merges with a track which drops sharply to Glen Feshie. From here, there are a number of options for returning to the start: the easiest is to follow tracks north through peaceful woodland to reach new forest. Keep left at every junction in the plantation to emerge at a high embankment. A good path leads along the top to reach a field. Cross this, aiming for the corner of another plantation. Cross by a stile to Auchlean, and return along the road (7h40).

◀ Looking north along lower Glen Feshie

45

A view of Loch Einich

Sgor Gaoith Ⓜ (1118m)

Walk time 5h20 Height gain 800m
Distance 14km OS Map Explorer 403

**A long climb through Caledonian forest
and along a bumpy ridge to reach a high
peak with fine views over Loch Einich
and Braeriach.**

Start 100m north of the bridge across the
Allt Ruadh at a large forestry clearing on
the road between Feshiebridge and
Auchlean (GR852013). Take the track east
through the plantation to a point where
several tracks converge. Continue eastwards
above the river by a good path which

climbs gradually through old forest. Where
the path drops to cross a tributary (the
Allt nan Bo), watch for a smaller trail on the
left. This climbs north through sparse forest
to reach a bealach and a small circular
shelter (GR876021). Climb steep rocky
slopes southeastwards to the top of Geal-
charn (2h20). Follow the ridgeline as it
curves southeast over a number of small
knolls before the final push south to the
summit ridge of Sgor Gaoith (GR903989)
(3h40). The south top is the highest, and
gives the best panorama over Loch Einich
and the great hulk of Braeriach beyond. To
descend, bear southwest for about 200m

and then drop west to what eventually becomes a vague ridge with a path. Trend northwest towards the waters of the Allt a'Chrom-alltain. Here, another path leads northwards above the glen and back to the start (5h20).

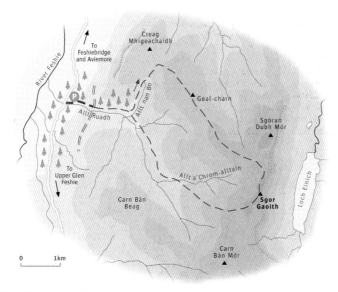

The Rothiemurchus Estate

The western boundary of the Rothiemurchus Estate runs along the tops of Creag Dhubh and Sgor Gaoith to include Loch Einich and Braeriach. Forestry plays a major part in the estate, with woodland occupying almost half of the 10,000ha. Commercial forestry is limited to a small area, as the estate has been committed to a programme of biodiversity and natural regeneration for many years and has one of the largest remnants of Caledonian pine forest in Scotland. The pine and oak forests are mixed with birch and juniper and often complemented by willow and alder to create diverse and healthy habitats.

◄ Creag Dhubh, above Gleann Einich, from Inverdruie

Up the Lairig Ghru

Braeriach (1296m)

Walk time 10h **Height gain** 1300m
Distance 30km **OS Map** Landranger 36

A long circuit which runs through the forests of the Rothiemurchus Estate to the high plateau of Braeriach and its hidden corries.

Start from the caravan park at Coylumbridge on the B970 (GR915106). Walk south on the track marked for the Lairig Ghru, which passes through a gate and forks soon after: take the path on the left which winds SSE through the forest for 2km to a track. Turn left, cross the Allt Druidh by the bridge and follow the burn upstream for 1.5km to a crossroads. Now turn right to follow the Lairig Ghru south as it gains gradual height above the river. This soon emerges into open country, leading you towards the steep pass and cliffs of Lurcher's Crag to the east. Leave the path here, ford the river and start to climb steeply southwest to join the humped north ridge of Sròn na Lairige: repair work has been carried out in places, making the ascent easier. Climb south to a cairn which marks the top of Sròn na Lairige (GR964006). Descend to a bealach, and climb west around the rim of the steep Coire Bhrochain to the summit of Braeriach (GR953998) (5h40). The view over to Cairn Toul is spectacular: the aptly named Lochan Uaine (Angel's Loch) hangs gracefully on the far side of the wild corrie. Continue west over the plateau for 1km, keeping to the high ground. Walk SSW over Einich Cairn, and drop south to find a narrow channel with a small burn. A path zigzags by the water into Coire Dhondail, and then leads northwards, losing altitude above Loch Einich, to reach an excellent track near the foot of the loch. Follow this north along Gleann Einich for about 4km to reach the start of the trees. Here, the track divides: keep to the river rather than climbing the hill. The tracks shortly converge and, after 2km, you reach an intersection at a small loch. Turn right to return northwards to Coylumbridge (10h).

Mountain races

Many adventure races are organised over the hills of the Highlands, often using ancient roads like the Lairig Ghru. A race is held along here in the summer, and runs the 45km from Braemar to Aviemore. The men's and women's records are both well under four hours for the arduous route which has 650m of ascent.

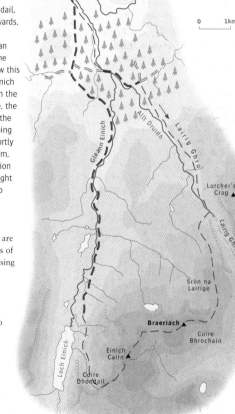

◀ The Angel's Peak from Braeriach

Meall a'Bhuachaille and the forest trail

Meall a'Bhuachaille **C** (810m)

Walk time 3h20 Height gain 500m
Distance 9km OS Map Explorer 403

**A short walk which begins in the
Queen's Forest and climbs a ridge with
good views over to Cairn Gorm and the
Northern Corries.**

Start from the Forestry Commission
Visitor Centre in Glenmore (GR977098).
A path, marked by posts with an orange
stripe, starts just left of the visitor centre

building and rises steeply through trees.
After 200m, the path forks. Turn left to
climb gently northwards by a burn through
a mixture of native woodland and
plantation. The burn leads the path through
a tangle of low branches and twisted roots
before emerging into the open where the
ground starts to steepen between the last
of the Caledonian pine. Continue to climb,
aiming for the east side of a bealach
between Creagan Gorm and Meall
a'Bhuachaille. Turn east, and ascend the

vague west ridge to the summit (GR991115) (1h40). Bear northeast across the plateau for 200m to find a path which descends directly east to Ryvoan Bothy, a good place to rest for a while if the weather is poor. A track leads southwest past An Lochan Uaine and along the Allt na Féith Duibhe to Glenmore Lodge. This leaves just a short walk back to the visitor centre at Glenmore (3h20).

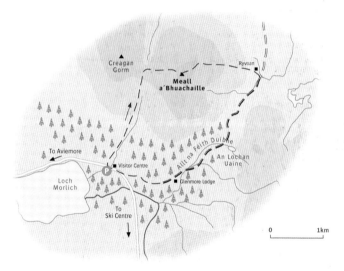

Bothies

In Scotland, a bothy, or *bothan* in Gaelic, used to be either the temporary quarters provided on a farm for unmarried male farm workers, or a remote rough hut for use by shepherds. 'Bothying' as a recreational activity began in the 1950s when hillwalking became popular and travel more affordable. The Mountain Bothy Association today restores and maintains many properties, and defines them as 'unlocked shelters in remote country for the use and benefit of all who love wild and lonely places'.

Bynack More by Strath Nethy

**Bynack More ⑩ (1090m),
A'Choinneach** (1017m)

Walk time 8h40 Height gain 800m
Distance 26km OS Map Landranger 36

**A walk over a less visited but
entertaining peak with great views into
the Loch A'an basin. The return along
Strath Nethy can be quite hard going.**

Start at Glenmore Lodge, the mountain
training centre for Sport Scotland
(GR986095). The lodge road continues
northeast as a track: follow it through
Caledonian pine and past the still waters of
An Lochan Uaine on the right. At a fork
beyond the edge of the forest, turn right to
follow signs for Braemar and climb gently

to gain the Garbh Allt at Bynack Stable, a
rough shelter in bad weather. Cross the
river, and continue southeast by the
renovated path which ascends a vague
ridge. Hold your course until you reach the
lower plateau of Bynack More. Leave the
path here, and bear due south over gentle
boggy slopes to the steepening main north
ridge. The crest provides some adventure:
climb over or around the dorsal plates of
this sleeping dinosaur to reach the summit
(GR042063) (4h). Descend due south to the
Barns of Bynack, a set of large boulders,
before bearing southwest over a flat
bealach to ascend A'Chòinneach. Continue
southwest, following the natural line of the
ridge over awkward, rocky ground to The

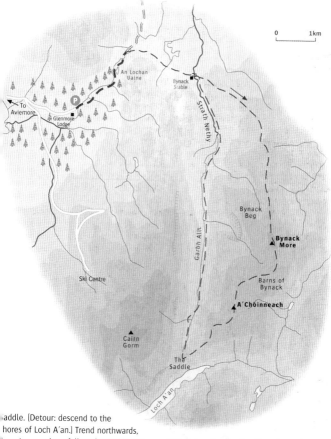

0   1km

An Lochan Uaine

Bynack Stable

To Aviemore

Glenmore Lodge

Strath Nethy

Bynack Beg

Bynack More ▲

Garbh Allt

Ski Centre

Barns of Bynack

A'Choinneach ▲

Cairn Gorm

The Saddle

Loch A'an

addle. [Detour: descend to the hores of Loch A'an.] Trend northwards, ropping gently to follow the Garbh Allt hrough Strath Nethy. The path is not vell-defined, particularly in the upper glen vhere a huge boulder field covers the west side, but as the strath widens the path along the east bank of the burn improves: this leads back to Bynack Stable. Retrace your steps to Glenmore Lodge (8h40).

Bynack More from the north

Cairn Gorm and the Northern Corries

Cairn Gorm ⓜ (1245m),
Cairn Lochan (1215m)

Walk time 5h40 Height gain 900m
Distance 14km OS Map Explorer 403

Easy access and good facilities make this area a big hit with climbers, walkers and skiers. The route skirts around two corries, which may create difficulties in bad weather.

Start from the large car park at Coire na Ciste, 2km before the main ski station (GR998074). Walk to the east end of the car park where the ski tow is visible. Cross the Allt na Ciste, and bear east to join a ridge which rises SSE: this becomes less pronounced as you gain height, but continue up steeper slopes until you reach the Cairngorm plateau. Climb over Cnap Coire na Spreidhe, which looks out on the Ptarmigan Restaurant and the ski runs of Coire Cas, to reach the summit tors and weather station of Cairn Gorm (GR005040) (2h20). Head west from the summit to a small knoll and boulder after 600m. [Escape: in poor visibility or high winds, it is advisable to descend northwest to the ski centre along the Fiacaill a'Choire Chais.] Good navigation is essential from this point, as the Northern Corries are steep: the edges cannot always be identified in mist and may be corniced in winter. Walk south to a rounded bealach, and rise gently to the high point above Coire an t-Sneachda before descending to another bealach. Climb west to the summit of Cairn Lochan

(GR985025) (3h40). From the top, descend SSW for 1km to avoid more cliffs and then north along an excellent ridge on the west side of Coire an Lochain. A path follows this ridge, crosses a burn and then drops gently northeast before joining another path from Coire an t-Sneachda which takes you to the ski centre. Walk back along the road to the start (5h40).

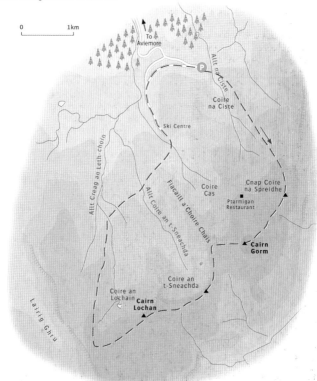

0   1km

To
Aviemore

P

Allt na Ciste

Coire
na Ciste

Ski Centre

Allt Creag an Leth-choin

Allt Coire an t-Sneachda

Fiacaill a Choire Chais

Coire
Cas

Cnap Coire
na Spreidhe

Ptarmigan
Restaurant

**Cairn
Gorm**

Coire an
t-Sneachda

Coire an
Lochain **Cairn
Lochan**

Lairig Ghru

◄ Coire an t-Sneachda

Along the Burn of Brown

Carn na Farraidh (688m)

Walk time 5h20 Height gain 400m
Distance 17km OS Map Landranger 36

A pleasant walk along two glens by good paths and tracks, with a short climb over moorland and a small river crossing close to the start.

Start at the path marked for Glen Brown, about 200m east of the bridge at Bridge of Brown (GR126204). Take the path southwards, passing through a small forest before climbing to a ruined farm building. Walk southeast over fields to reach Stronachavie, another ruin hidden behind the brow of the hill. Pass through a gate on the south side of the building, and take the track which soon starts to drop west to reach a large plantation by the Burn of Brown. Cross to the west bank, and follow the river southwards by a grassy track. Before the end of the plantation, a smaller burn joins from the west. Climb the steep embankment between the two burns, passing a few trees, to emerge on a good gravel track bearing southwards. After about 400m, where the track contours eastwards around the hill, take a smaller track which descends from the south. This climbs through heather, fading where the ground levels out. Tramp southeast across the featureless bog before rising to the summit of Carn na Farraidh, which is scored with gullies (GR114148) (2h40). Descend southwest off the hill to reach a new track. Follow this for about 3.5km until midway

between a gate leading to Upper Dell and the plantations of Dorback Lodge. Another track rises northeast to reach the croft of Fae after 1km. Continue northwards, keeping to the flat ground at first and then descending by the Allt Iomadaidh to a peaceful glen. After dropping to ford

a small tributary, climb gently northeast along a grassy track to emerge on the road above Bridge of Brown (5h20). Reward yourself with cakes in the tearoom.

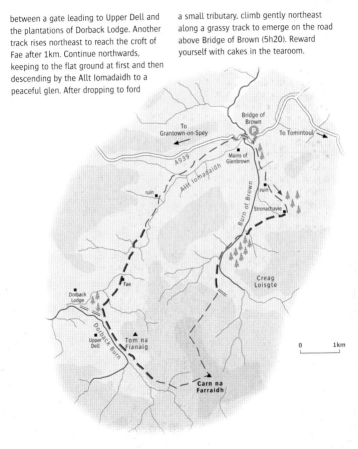

◀ The northern Cairngorms from near Bridge of Brown

Cromdale Coronation

Creagan a'Chaise (722m),
Carn a Ghille Chearr (710m)

Walk time 6h20 Height gain 900m
Distance 19km OS Map Landranger 36

A ridge walk that overlooks the patchwork of fields and forests between the straths of Spey and Avon. The route can be boggy in places.

Start from the car park on the west side of the bridge off the B9136 at Mains of Inverourie (GR154266). Walk SSW along the minor road on the west bank of the Avon for about 2.5km to reach The Milton, a farmhouse by a lone pine tree. A gate opposite the house gives access to a track that rises westwards. After 300m, cross down to and over Milton Burn to follow the wide track more steeply westwards. Near a stalkers' hut, the track disappears: keep climbing westwards over the heather to the top of Creagan a'Chaise and its magnificent Jubilee Cairn of 1887 (GR104242) (2h40). Descend northwards to follow the main ridge. After about 2km, you will reach a hillock with a pointed cairn which marks the spot of a huge bonfire held for the coronation of Edward VII and Queen Alexandra in 1902. Drop northeast from the cairn before climbing the wide ridge to the top of Carn Eachie. The terrain is pretty flat from here to the summit of Carn a Ghille Chearr (GR139299) (5h). Descend southeast over heather slopes, keeping the Allt na Ha just to the right: the ground is steep at first but soon relents. Lower down, aim for the north end of a birch wood to cross a fence by a gate. Keep the trees on the right to reach another gate close to the farmhouse of Lyne. A track serves the house and fords the burn (there is also a footbridge here) before passing the cottage of Alltnaha.

Continue along the track, which drops to meet the Avon and leads directly to the start point (6h20).

The Wolf of Badenoch

Born in 1343, Alexander Stewart was the fourth illegitimate son of King Robert II and a grandson of Robert the Bruce. Irreligious and barbaric, even by the standards of the time, the Wolf was frequently in dispute with the Bishop of Moray and was excommunicated after destroying Elgin Cathedral in 1390. Understandably, he was feared throughout the Highlands and many legends surround the evil Wolf and his stronghold, the bleak island castle of Lochindorb on Dava Moor, north of Grantown-on-Spey. Appropriately, Lochindorb means 'loch of trouble'.

◄ Looking west from the summit of Creagan a'Chaise

Braemar lies at the heart of the Cairngorms, surrounded by high peaks. At 320m above sea level, it is the highest parish in Britain. In spite of its popularity with summer visitors, the village has retained its douce character and modern developments have been kept to a minimum. Braemar's two castles give some clue to its ancient royal connections, and it is home to the annual Braemar Gathering patronised by the Queen.

The hills of Braemar are encircled by high mountains, which form the borders for the other four regions in this guide. The main road that sweeps in along the Clunie Water from Glen Shee and out by the Dee towards Ballater represents the only vehicular access. There are plenty of choices, however, for walkers and cyclists, including Jock's Road from Glen Clova, the Lairig Ghru from Aviemore and routes from Glen Tilt or Glen Feshie.

Many of the walks in this section are approached using these old paths and tracks. To the south of Braemar, one walk starts

along Jock's Road with another to The Cairnwell returning through Glen Baddoch. Two routes are reached from Glen Ey, just west of Braemar. Three long routes start from the Linn of Dee: a horseshoe on Ben Macdui; a circuit to The Angel's Peak; and a walk into the Loch A'an basin. This section also includes a gentle walk on Braemar's own hill, Morrone.

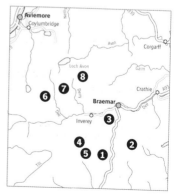

Hills of Braemar

Baddoch Burn Circuit

Carn Aosda Ⓜ (917m), **The Cairnwell** Ⓜ
(933m), **Carn nan Sac** (920m),
Carn a'Gheòidh Ⓜ (975m)

Walk time 6h + detour 40 min
Height gain 700m
Distance 17km OS Map Landranger 43

**A walk over several mountains in the
popular Glen Shee skiing area, with a
peaceful descent through Glen Baddoch.**

Start at the small track to Baddoch on the
south side of a plantation (GR138833).
(Parking places on the A93: do not block
access to Baddoch.) Cross the stile, and
follow the track west over a bridge.

Immediately after crossing the river, turn off
the track and climb diagonally southwest to
attain the ridge of Strone Baddoch. An old
track weaves its way slowly southwards to
Carn Chrionaidh. Keep to the high ground
from here, and bear east to reach the
summit of Carn Aosda with its ski tows and
drift fences (GR134792) (2h20). Retrace
steps for about 200m to join a track which
descends southwards to a bealach, and then
climb by fences to a flat area above a ski
tow. [Detour: continue southeast along the
track to the jumble of cables and structures
that mark the summit of The Cairnwell.
Return the same way (add 40 min).]

Descend west to a small bealach and then climb southwest, following the easy crest of the ridge to Carn nan Sac. Continue westwards to the summit of Carn a'Gheòidh (GR107767) (3h40). Descend gently northwest for 1km, and then take the broad north spur into a verdant glen. Follow the waters downstream, cross to the west bank of the river by a hidden footbridge, and join the track which leads back to Baddoch (6h).

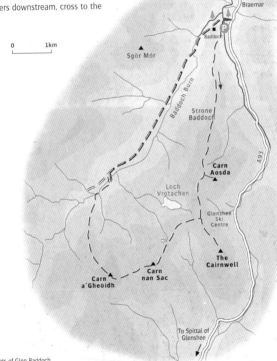

Jock's Road and Glen Callater

Carn an Tuirc Ⓜ (1019m), **Cairn of Claise** Ⓜ
(1064m), **Tom Buidhe** Ⓜ (957m),
Tolmount Ⓜ (958m)

Walk time 6h + detour 40 min
Height gain 800m
Approach and return 1h bike or 2h40 walk
Distance 16km + 10km approach and return
OS Maps Landranger 43 and 44

**A journey over tops around the
atmospheric Coire Loch Kander,
descending by an historic path. Use of a
mountain bike will reduce access time.**

Start from Auchallater, where the road
crosses the Callater Burn 3km south of
Braemar (GR156882). (Good parking here.)
Take the track marked for Glen Clova, and
follow the burn 5km upstream to
Lochcallater Lodge. Leave bikes here: walk
times start from this point. Cross the river,
and follow the west shore of the loch for
200m to the obvious track that climbs due
south. Further up, this joins the northeast
spur of Carn an Tuirc above Coire Loch
Kander. Climb gently to the summit of Carn
an Tuirc, situated to the far west of the
plateau. Walk due east to the bealach to
rejoin the path near the edge of the corrie.
Continue southwards over the gentle terrain
of Cairn of Claise to find a long wall: follow

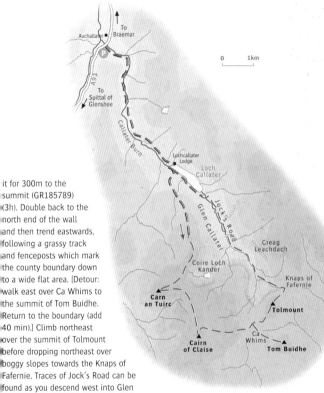

it for 300m to the summit (GR185789) (3h). Double back to the north end of the wall and then trend eastwards, following a grassy track and fenceposts which mark the county boundary down to a wide flat area. [Detour: walk east over Ca Whims to the summit of Tom Buidhe. Return to the boundary (add 40 min).] Climb northeast over the summit of Tolmount before dropping northeast over boggy slopes towards the Knaps of Fafernie. Traces of Jock's Road can be found as you descend west into Glen Callater: good cairns mark the route but the ground is often rough. The path soon reaches the base of the glen and follows the river on its east bank. Lower down, the glen opens up to accommodate Loch Callater: ford the river to join a good track which leads along the west shore of the loch and back to the lodge (6h). [Variant: to avoid the river crossing, continue on the east shore of the loch to the lodge.] Return to the start.

◀ Distant peaks of Glen Callater from the southwest

65

Morrone of Braemar

Morrone (859m)

**Walk time 4h40 Height gain 500m
Distance 14km OS Map Landranger 43**

**A route from Braemar which gives
excellent views along Upper Glen Dee,
and returns through ancient forest of
birch and juniper.**

Start from the Fife Arms Hotel at the centre of Braemar (GR150914). From opposite the hotel, take the minor road south past the church to the golf course. Just before the clubhouse, a path climbs west through a small fixed caravan site. Cross a stile into woodland and exit by a gate where a sign welcomes you into the nature reserve. Take the path southwest up the bare slopes of

Morrone: this climbs at the same gradient for some time until you meet five cairns. Continue over easier slopes to the summit (GR132886) (2h). Descend SSW by the wide track to a knoll. Here, the track trends southeast: leave it to drop southwest over undulating ground, keeping north of Coire nam Freumh to reach and cross the Corriemulzie Burn. A good gravel track descends with ease on the west bank to reach a bridge after 2.5km. Do not enter the plantation after the bridge, but leave the track to follow paths around the west side of the forest. After passing a broken dam, you will emerge on the road between Braemar and Inverey. Walk towards Braemar for 600m, passing two houses on the right

and one on the left. Immediately before the parking area on the left, take the fenced track on the right which runs parallel to the road. Follow this over a stile and into forest, and turn right at the first junction. After a steady ascent of 500m, turn left onto a minor grassy track which crosses a small burn after 800m before coming to another fork. Turn right here to reach a stile at the edge of the plantation. This leads to the Birkwood Nature Reserve. After 1.5km, a fence leads to a junction: turn left and head north down the track past Tomintoul and into Braemar (4h40).

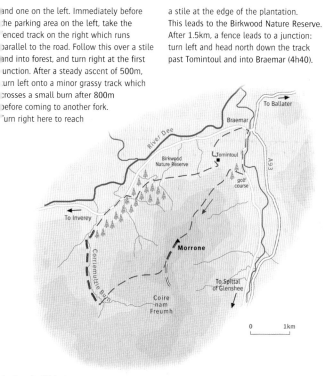

The bonnie birkin tree

The National Nature Reserve, administered by Scottish Natural Heritage, on the lower slopes of Morrone is one of the best examples of an upland birch (birk) wood in Britain. A dense understory of juniper and many lime-loving herbs also flourish in this unusual woodland, estimated from pollen preserved in the peat bed to be more than 8000 years old.

The River Dee by Morrone

The Battery Top

Carn Creagach (894m),
Carn Bhac Ⓜ (946m),
Top of the Battery (784m)

Walk time 6h40 Height gain 800m
Distance 20km OS Map Landranger 43

A ridge walk over rolling terrain which gives great views south into Glen Tilt or north to the Lairig Ghru.

Start from the parking area about 200m west of the memorial in Inverey (GR089893). A track rises southwards to serve a group of houses. After 200m, in front of a lodge, the track forks: continue straight ahead to a low gate by a clump of trees. This track follows the river along Glen Ey, and crosses by a bridge before gaining height above the water. After about 3km, beyond the ruin and a small bridge across the Allt an t-Sionnaich, leave the glen to climb southwards over heather slopes. These begin to relent as they become the northeast ridge of Creag an Lochain. From the top, the walking eases considerably. Continue southwest to a higher point at Carn Creagach. Drop west to a boggy bealach, and climb the featureless slopes which steepen towards the summit of Carn Bhac (GR051832) (4h). Descend WSW to follow the ridge for 1km to a subsidiary top. From here, descend north along a prominent ridge. The terrain, which is bogg

◀ Geal Charn from Carn Bhac

in places, leads northeast to the Top of the Battery: the long narrow escarpment just below the summit is visible from afar. Continue northeast down the steepening ridge to the glen. When you reach flatter ground, walk north to ford the Allt Cristie Mór and climb the banks to reach the excellent track above. Follow this down to Loin-a-veaich and the road at Inverey (6h40).

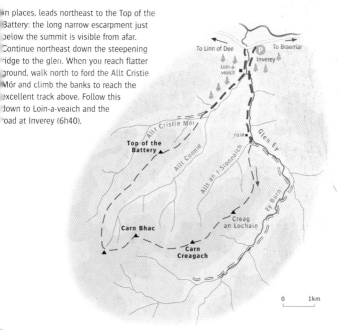

The Braemar Gathering

The Braemar Gathering is held every year on the first Saturday in September. It is an event with a rich history, reputedly instigated by King Malcolm III (Canmore) (1031-1093), who defeated and killed MacBeth at the Battle of Lumphanan. It was common in the middle ages to have gatherings of clan chiefs and warriors who would organise a hunt and compete at various games to test speed, strength and fighting skills. The Invergarry Games in 1820 included a contest to twist the four legs off a cow, for which a sheep was offered as a prize. Modern Highland Games are more likely to feature running, jumping, hammer-throwing and tossing the caber, as well as piping and dancing competitions.

Glen Ey and beyond

An Socach (ⓜ)(944m), **Carn an Righ** (ⓜ)
(1029m), **Màm nan Carn** (986m),
Beinn Iutharn Mhór (ⓜ)(1045m)

Walk time 6h + detour 1h
Height gain 1100m
Approach and return 2h bike or 4h walk
Distance 16km + 16km approach and return
OS Map Landranger 43

**A demanding circuit over high rounded
peaks in remote country. A mountain
bike gives the best access to the start.**

Start from the parking area about 200m
west of the memorial in Inverey
(GR089893). A track rises southwards to
serve a group of houses. After 200m, in
front of a lodge, the track forks: continue
straight ahead to a low gate by a clump of
trees. This track follows the river along Glen
Ey, and crosses by a bridge before gaining
height above the water. After 8km, you will
come to the ruined Altanour Lodge. Leave
bikes here: walk times start from this point.
At the southeast corner of a dismal forest, a
hidden footbridge spans the chasm of the
River Ey. Cross here, and walk upstream
over heather for about 1km before
beginning your ascent of the steep north
ridge of An Socach. The ground eases
towards the summit (1h40) (GR079799).
As you descend SSE, steep scree soon gives
way to undulating moorland. Continue
southwards to gain the long ridge of Carn
a'Chlarsaich which is followed westwards
over several small tops to its summit.
Descend west to Loch nan Eun, skirting
around the water on the south side and
passing the remains of a shieling, and then

◀ The path to Carn an Righ

bear WSW over the watershed and into Gleann Mór. A path soon leads easily above the glen to a bealach between Carn an Righ and Màm nan Carn: on a good day The Devil's Point and Cairn Toul can be seen from here. [Detour: climb west, and then northwest over the rounded mass of Carn an Righ to its summit. Return the same way (add 1h).] Climb northeast along a well-defined ridge: the terrain eases towards the summit of Màm nan Carn. Descend northwest before the last climb of the day, this time to the summit of Beinn Iutharn Mhór (GR045793) (4h40). Drop gently eastwards to a knoll, and then north to another with a cairn to find the excellent northeast ridge

which leads down to Glen Ey. Lower down, where the ridge steepens, a path makes a clever zigzag descent before fading out. Follow deer tracks above the Allt Beinn Iutharn (you will be lucky if you find the stalkers' path through the heather) to join a track near the old lodge (6h). Return to Inverey.

71

The Angel and the Devil

The Devil's Point Ⓜ (1004m), **Cairn Toul** Ⓜ (1291m), **Sgor an Lochain Uaine** (The Angel's Peak) Ⓜ (1258m), **Monadh Mór** Ⓜ (1113m), **Beinn Bhrotain** Ⓜ (1157m)

Walk time 10h40 Height gain 1400m
Approach and return 1h bike or 2h40 walk
Distance 32km + 10km approach and return
OS Map Landranger 43

A long and challenging walk along the Lairig Ghru to the remote corries of Cairn Toul or over The Devil's Point, with a return across the high tops. Cycling in will save some time on approach.

Start at the Linn of Dee car park (GR063897). Walk or cycle west along a good track on the north bank of the River Dee for 5km to the White Bridge. Bikes can be left here: walk times start from this point. Instead of crossing the bridge, follow a good path upstream on the northeast bank of the Dee. The commanding spectacle of The Devil's Point draws nearer as you walk north up the glen. After 9km, a bridge spans the river to Corrour Bothy which dates from 1877. Keep to the west bank of the Dee as you circumnavigate Cairn Toul over uneven ground, and then follow the Allt a'Garbh Choire to a roughly built shelter. From here, ascend a faint path steeply southwards to reach the artfully moulded Lochan Uaine. Climb the rocky east flank of the cirque directly to the summit of Cairn Toul (GR963972) (5h). [Variant: leave Corrour due west along a path which rises steeply to a bealach. Climb to The Devil's Point and return to the bealach. Follow the rim of Coire Odhar and Coire an t-Saighdeir to the summit of Cairn Toul.] Descend west, staying close to the rim of the corrie, to a bealach and cairn and then climb even slopes to the summit

◀ The Lairig Ghru near Corrour

of The Angel's Peak. Drop SSW, keeping close to the corrie edge for 500m until the southwest ridge allows easy progress to a wide bealach above Loch nan Stuirteag.

[Escape: walk southeast to the loch before descending steep and sometimes boggy slopes to Glen Geusachan. Follow the Dee south to join a track to the White Bridge.] Bear southeast over steep terrain, which levels out towards the rounded summit of Monadh Mór. Continue south before dropping sharply southeast by a good path to a bealach. Maintain this course as you climb at first by a path and then over slabs to the summit of Beinn Bhrotain (GR954923) (8h40). Descend eastwards to reach the start of a burn that trickles through Coire an t-Sneachda. This becomes the Allt Garbh which is easily followed to a track on the west side of Glen Dee. Follow the River Dee downstream to the White Bridge (10h40). Walk or cycle back to the start.

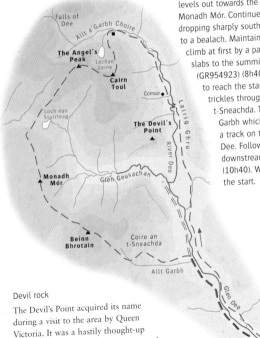

Devil rock

The Devil's Point acquired its name during a visit to the area by Queen Victoria. It was a hastily thought-up alternative to avoid embarrassment as the Gaelic name of *Bod an Deamhain* translates as 'The Devil's Penis'.

Ben Macdui

Derry Cairngorm ⓜ(1155m),
Ben Macdui ⓜ(1309m),
Carn a'Mhaim ⓜ(1037m)

Walk time 7h40 Height gain 1400m
Approach and return 1h bike or 2h40 walk
Distance 21km + 10km approach and return
OS Map Landranger 43

An unusual horseshoe over the highest peak in the Cairngorms. Navigation skills would be useful as the plateau is often cloaked in mist. A mountain bike will give quick access into Glen Derry.

Start at the Linn of Dee car park (GR063897). Follow the signs for Glen Lui into the forest and across a boardwalk to join a track. This follows the Lui Water for 5km upstream to Derry Lodge. Leave bikes here: walk times start from this point. Cross the footbridge just after the large shed, and follow a path northwest through Caledonian forest. This soon steepens, exits the trees and skirts around the crags of Creag Bad an t-Seabhaig. Continue more easily up the ridge towards Carn Crom. The path navigates this peak via an exposed path on the east side. Walk northwards over gently sloping ground to the summit of Derry Cairngorm (GR017980) (2h40). Descend northwest to reach a bealach. Instead of continuing over Creagan a'Choire Etchachan, drop easily southwest into Coire Sputan Dearg. Climb steeply towards the central section of the crags where a huge inverted V is notched into the rock, and drop down to the solitude of Lochan Uaine. From the foot of the loch, take a rising traverse southwards for about 300m to meet Sròn Riach, the southeast ridge of Ben Macdui. Climb steeply

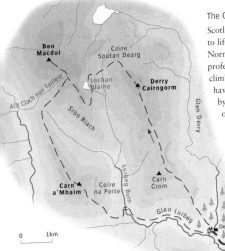

The Old Grey Man of Ben Macdui

Scotland's answer to the Yeti came to life over a century ago when Norman Collie, a chemistry professor, wrote an article in a climbing journal. He claimed to have been chased off Ben Macdui by a large shadowy figure. Many other climbers have since claimed similar experiences and the myth has grown. Collie was a well-known practical joker, however, as well as being the inventor of the neon bulb.

northwest through broken rock and then over easier ground, keeping the edge of the corrie within sight. Once you gain the plateau, bear WNW to the summit of Ben Macdui (GR988989) (4h40). Return ESE along the plateau for about 800m, and then drop southwest along a vague ridge. Maintain your course to reach a bealach between Ben Macdui and Carn a'Mhaim. From here, the defined ridge of Carn a'Mhaim with its several false tops leads you to the summit. Descend southwest by a reasonable path, making sure you keep to the south side of the rocky Coire na Poite. This path drops steeply to the floor of Glen Luibeg before joining a path from the Lairig

Ghru. Pass through a gate, and either walk 300m north to the footbridge or ford the Luibeg Burn here. The path continues from the other side of the burn to Derry Lodge (7h40). Return to Linn of Dee.

◄ The glen of the Allt Carn a'Mhaim from Ben Macdui

Glen Derry to Loch A'an

Beinn Bhreac (m)(931m),
Beinn a'Chaorainn (m)(1082m),
Beinn Mheadhoin (m)(1182m)

Walk time 8h + detours 2h
Height gain 1000m
Approach and return 1h bike or 2h40 walk
Distance 25km + 10km approach and return
OS Map Landranger 43

A long and rewarding circuit into the heart of the Cairngorms. A mountain bike will speed access into Glen Derry.

Start at the Linn of Dee car park (GR063897). Follow the signs for Glen Lui into the forest and across a boardwalk to join a track. This follows the Lui Water for 5km upstream to Derry Lodge. Leave bikes here: walk times start from this point. Cross the footbridge just after the large shed, and follow a path northwards through delightful Caledonian forest. After 3km, at the edge of the forest, a bridge takes you to the east bank. Continue on the path for about 500m and then, soon after passing a small clump of trees on the right, leave it to climb NNE over heather and bog. This becomes the rounded ridge of Coire an Fhir Bhogha, which is followed to the flat top of Craig Derry. [Detour: walk southeast to the double top of Beinn Bhreac. The eastern summit is higher by a few metres. Return to Craig Derry (add 40 min).] Head northeast, keeping to the highest and driest ground around the featureless moor of Mòine Bhealaidh, and then climb NNW over firmer ground to the summit of Beinn a'Chaorainn (GR045013) (3h20). Descend north to gain a prominent, rocky ridge. When the ridge loses definition after about 1km, drop westwards into the Lairig an Laoigh. Ford the burn, and take a path which leads to the River Avon before continuing upstream on the south bank. After about 600m, where the river flows with more force, climb the steep moraine banks

◄ Loch A'an from below
Shelter Stone Crag

to gain a boggy
path that bears west
into the Loch A'an
basin: this is dominated
by the enormous Shelter
Stone Crag. Continue for 3km
to the head of the loch where
huge boulders carved from the
cliff create natural shelters from bad
weather (a renowned bivouac spot
among mountaineers). Leave the basin
on a good path, which starts at some
rounded knolls and climbs steeply
south before easing just short of
Loch Etchachan. [Detour: to climb
Beinn Mheadhoin, leave the path and
ascend gritty slopes northeast until
the ridge levels off, then continue over
easier ground. Three tors, each bigger than
the one before, mark the trail to the summit
(GR024017). Return to Loch Etchachan (add
1h20).] Cross the burn at the foot of the loch
and take the path that descends southeast,
passing the Hutchison Memorial Hut before
entering Glen Derry. Cross the Glas Allt Mór
(this may be difficult to ford in spate), and
continue through the glen to Derry Lodge
(8h). Return to Linn of Dee.

This section covers Deeside, Donside and Avonside, a large region that extends southeast to the Forest of Birse and north to Tomintoul. The dark cliffs of Lochnagar and the high plateau of Ben Avon at the centre present a different picture of the region from the undulating terrain of the peripheral mountains.

As one of Scotland's premier whisky distilling areas, the glens of the northeast Cairngorms are home to the well-known brands of Cardhu, Glenlivet and Glenfiddich. In the past the Smugglers' Trail, an infamous mountain route, saw countless barrels of *uisge beatha* transported from illicit stills in Speyside to the coast and the cities of the south. Today, a more civilised whisky trail directs aficionados around Aberdeenshire to sample the malts.

The Crown also has connections with the region: the Royal Estate of Balmoral and the Glenlivet Crown Estate contain large swathes of land, and there are many castles and stately homes to visit.

This section contains two high routes that start from Glen Muick near Ballater, and a

circuit on Beinn a'Bhuird that begins close to Braemar. The reclusive Ben Avon is approached from Tomintoul while Mount Keen involves a long bike ride through Glen Tanar. There are shorter walks in the Forest of Birse to the south and from Tomnavoulin. The Ladder Hills are the historic setting for a final route.

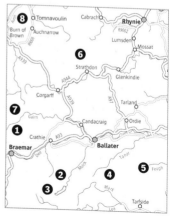

Whisky Country

Corries of Beinn a'Bhuird

Beinn a'Bhuird 🔟 (1197m)

Walk time 5h20 Height gain 900m
Approach and return 1h40 bike or 4h walk
Distance 15km + 17km approach and return
OS Maps Landranger 36 and 43

**A great mountain with the classic
scooped-out corries and sheared cliffs
of glacial erosion. In mist, precise
navigation is essential for the descent.
This route is best approached by
mountain bike.**

Start from the Keiloch Estate by the
Bridge of Dee on the A93, 4km east of
Braemar (GR187912). (Park at the estate
entrance.) Follow signs for the Linn of
Quoich, pass the north side of Alltdourie
and take the second forestry track on the
right marked for Slugain. This soon reaches
a gate: cross by the stile and continue for
4km along the Allt an t-Slugain. Leave

bikes where the glen narrows and the track
becomes a path: walk times start from this
point. Follow the path through an
enchanting gorge to reach an old ruin. Pass
over the watershed to gain the first views of
the peak, and then bear north to keep
above the Quoich Water on a good but
sometimes boggy path: this gives
increasingly good views of the crags of
Beinn a'Bhuird. Cross the Glas Allt Mór
where the glen steepens below Ben Avon,
and climb north for a short distance to
reach Clach a'Cléirich (the Clerk's Boulder).
Leave the path here to climb northwest up
steep heathery slopes. These relent before
the final haul to the rocky top of the ridge.
Continue westwards, following the high
ground to reach the North Top (GR092006)
(3h20). Care should be taken in navigating
this mountain: the cliffs may be overhung
with cornices in winter or obscured in mist.

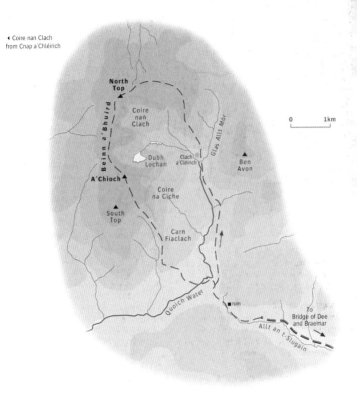

◀ Coire nan Clach
from Cnap a'Chléirich

0   1km

North
Top

Coire
nan
Clach

Glas Allt Mòr

Dubh
Lochan

Clach
a'Chléirich

Ben
Avon

A'Chioch

Coire
na Cìche

South
Top

Carn
Fiaclach

Quoich Water

ruin

To
Bridge of Dee
and Braemar

Allt an t-Slugain

Head SSW over the plateau to the tors of A'Chioch and then southeast, passing close to the edge of Coire na Cìche with its shield of slabs. Descend steeply southeast over the boulders of a prominent rib to reach a small bealach before Carn Fiaclach. A narrow path drops south on the west side of the ridge and then east across moorland. Hop across the Quoich Water, and walk eastwards to rejoin the original path. Glen an t-Slugain appears suddenly, hidden as it is from the west. Continue past the ruin and along the widening glen (5h20). Return to the start.

Dark Lochnagar

Lochnagar: Cac Carn Beag ⓜ (1155m)

Walk time 7h Height gain 800m
Distance 20km OS Map Landranger 44

**A popular peak with a photogenic
northern corrie that has become a
favourite with mountaineers. This
route can be combined with the next
walk for an even longer challenge.**

Start from the large car park at the Spittal
of Glenmuick (GR310850), 11km southwest
of Ballater. Walk along the road to the
visitor centre, and then take a signposted
track northwest across the floor of the glen

towards the house at Allt na-giubhsaich.
Follow a path through the woods to
join the track that climbs westwards by a
burn. After about 3km, the track levels off
and contours north around the hill. Watch
for a good path that drops down on the
west side. This climbs even slopes to the
bealach near Meikle Pap, a point that
gives fine views of the steep buttresses
and gullies of Lochnagar: particularly
prominent is the rockfall scar on Parallel
Buttress which has collapsed several times
in recent years. Climb south along the ridge
over large boulders, and then follow the rim

◄ Pinnacle Face and Black Spout Buttress on Lochnagar

of the corrie (care is needed in poor visibility) to a large tor and cairn at Cac Carn Mór. The summit tor of Cac Carn Beag is only 500m north over the plateau (GR244862) (4h). Return to Cac Carn Mór, and descend southeastwards along a path which shortly begins to follow the Glas Allt. After a level stretch, the path enters a steep ravine with a waterfall and zigzags by the west side of the burn to reach Loch Muick at Glas-allt-Shiel. Follow the track along the west shore for 3km to the head of the loch. A path leads east to a track on the far side of the glen. This can be followed back to the Spittal (7h).

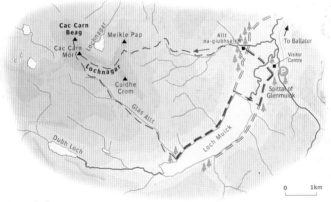

Literary Lochnagar

England thy beauties are tame and domestic / To one who has roved o'er the mountains afar/ Oh for the crags that are wild and majestic / The steep frowning glories of dark Lochnagar! 'Mad, Bad and Dangerous' Lord Byron, only son of 'Mad Jack' Byron by his second marriage to the Scottish heiress Catherine Gordon of Gight, spent his formative years in Aberdeenshire and climbed Lochnagar at the age of fifteen. Lochnagar also has many royal connections. Queen Victoria attempted an ascent on her pony in 1861 and *The Old Man of Lochnagar*, a successful children's book featuring underwater haggis who revolve as they swim and the miniature green people of Gorm, was written by Prince Charles in the 1980s.

Creag an Dubh-loch and Loch Muick

Carn a'Choire Bhaidheach ⓜ(1110m),
Carn an t-Sagairt Beag (1044m), **Carn an t-Sagairt Mór** ⓜ(1047m), **Cairn Bannoch** ⓜ
(1012m), **Broad Cairn** ⓜ(998m)

Walk time 9h Height gain 900m
Distance 28km OS Map Landranger 44

A long ridge walk over many tops, combined with a circuit of a stunning loch and a passage beneath the famous cliffs of Creag an Dubh-loch.

Start from the large car park at the Spittal of Glenmuick, 11km southwest of Ballater (GR310850). Walk along the road to the visitor centre, and then continue southwest up the wide glen. After 1km, take the path on the right which cuts across the glen along the foot of Loch Muick. This joins another track on the far side. Follow this along the west shore for 3km to the house at Glas-allt-Shiel before continuing to the head of the loch. Take a path from here to climb the hillside above Allt an Dubh-loch, eventually reaching Dubh Loch which is overshadowed by dramatic cliffs: those on the south side are a favourite with rock climbers. Continue past the loch, below an impressive waterfall by Eagles Rock. Beyond the last of the cliffs, climb northwards up heather slopes to reach the flat summit of Carn a'Choire Bhaidheach (GR227845) (4h40). Descend northwest a short way, and arc westwards over the highest ground to Carn an t-Sagairt Beag before dropping southwest to climb its bigger cousin, Carn an t-Sagairt Mór. Drop southeast to a rounded bealach shared with Fafernie, and then ascend the rocky summit of Cairn Bannoch (GR223825). Continue southeast along the ridge to the last summit of Broad Cairn (GR240815) (6h40). Descend the wide east ridge to gain a stony track which leads to a steading. Continue east for a further 300m and watch for a small renovated path on the left which bears

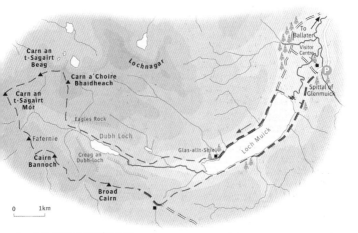

northeast across the moor. This is an excellent way down into the Loch Muick basin. Once by the shores, follow a path on the south side through inspiring scenery. Halfway along the loch, the path crosses a bridge and becomes a track. Follow this back to the Spittal (9h).

▼ Loch Muick close to the Spittal of Glenmuick

Mount Keen by the Mounth Road

Mount Keen Ⓜ (939m)

Walk time 4h20 Height gain 800m
Approach and return 2h bike or 4h20 walk
Distance 11km + 20km approach and return
OS Map Landranger 44

**A long journey through beautiful Scots
pine to reach some secluded hills. Use
of a mountain bike is recommended for
access up the glen.**

Start from the Braeloine car park in Glen
Tanar, 2.5km west of Bridge o'Ess
(GR480966). Walk or cycle southwest along
the road, following it around the equestrian
centre after 1km. A sign directs hikers past
a farm to a gate. Just beyond, a track leads
to a T-junction at the edge of the forest.

Turn left and follow signs for Glen Esk: an
excellent track leads WSW up the glen. At
Etnach a bridge crosses the river, and
another crosses back after 1km. Leave bikes
here: walk times start from this point.
Continue upstream over the rough ground
of the east bank if the river is in spate, or
along the track on the west if the water
level is low (and then cross back after
1.2km at a shieling and remains of an old
bridge). Climb south along the Mounth
Road, which starts as a wide gravel track
and later splits into two paths: both lead to
the ridge. The walking eases along the ridge
before steepening for the last 1km to the
summit of Mount Keen (GR409869) (2h20).
Descend east from the summit, steeply at

◄ Gathering Cairn from Mount Keen

first and then more easily, to reach a bealach. Follow a path northeast to the summit of Braid Cairn with its large obelisk marked with a B. Descend WNW, and follow the north ridge to Gathering Cairn. Drop northeast over awkward heather slopes to meet a track at a bealach. Follow this north to a junction before Black Craig. Turn left to return to the river and the bridge (4h20). Walk or cycle back along the Glen.

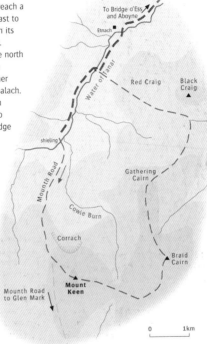

Granite and grouse

The dominant rock type in the Cairngorm massif is granite and, as a result, the soils are acidic, coarse and low in nutrients. Other rocks are also present, including schist which gives a richer, more fertile soil. It is not the best area in Scotland for arctic and alpine species in terms of variety, but there is often an abundance of certain local species where conditions are just right. The infertility of the granite soils has led to much of the Cairngorms being populated by red deer and grouse rather than sheep, which are choosier with their greens.

Fungle and Firmounth

Tampie (723m), **Gannoch** (731m)

Walk time 5h40 Height gain 500m
Distance 18km OS Map Landranger 44

**An undemanding journey which follows
paths and old tracks over rolling
grouse country.**

Start at a small chapel in Forest of Birse
at the end of the minor public road from
Finzean (GR533906). Take the track west,
following signs for Glen Esk, to reach the
farmhouse at Ballochan. Pass through a
gate, and bear west across the field for
300m to cross the Burn of Auldmad at a
hidden footbridge. From here, the excellent
Fungle Road leads SSW along the west side
of a burn. This track deteriorates after about

4km, but continue to climb towards the
west side of a bealach where the path
widens again. At an obelisk, ascend
heathery slopes due west for about 400m in
distance to reach a new track. This is the
Firmounth Road which runs all of the way
to Glen Tanar. Follow it northwards, passing
many well-built cairns, to the top of Tampie
(GR497868) (3h). The descent takes you
past a small lochan. Follow the
westernmost track by high fenceposts to a
prominent cairn marked WE1814, and then
walk east to the rounded top of Gannoch.
Descend northwest to rejoin the main path,
continuing to lose height for some distance
before climbing towards the top of
Craigmahandle (GR488906) (4h).

On the north side of the hill, there is a nature reserve sign and a new track. Instead of following this, leave the Firmounth Road and descend NNE by a small path to a boggy dip before climbing towards Hill of Duchery. A track takes you from the south side of the hill past several grouse butts to a junction where signs lead you away from the private grounds of Birse Castle. Go straight on, crossing another track, and descending the west side of a fenced field to the river. A path follows the water, crosses it by a footbridge and continues towards the forest. Jump over the stile, and pass through a field to find the first footbridge. It is only a short way back to the start (5h40).

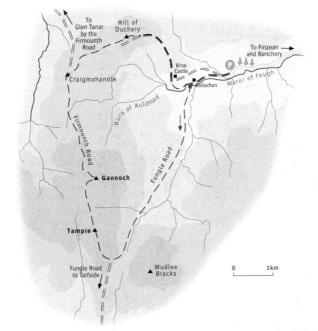

To Glen Tanar by the Firmounth Road

Hill of Duchery

To Finzean and Banchory

Birse Castle

P

Ballochan

Water of Feugh

Craigmahandle

Burn of Auldmad

Firmounth Road

Fungle Road

▲ Gannoch

Tampie ▲

Fungle Road to Tarfside

Mudlee Bracks ▲

0   1km

◄ Along the Fungle Road towards Birse Castle

Strathdon and the Ladder Hills

Little Geal Charn (742m),
Carn Mór C (804m)

Walk time 6h20 Height gain 600m
Distance 20km OS Map Landranger 37

**A circuit in the quiet country around
the Ladder Hills on tracks and over
a rough landscape of heather and
peat hags.**

Start at a break in the trees on the
road from Strathdon to Glenbuchat Lodge,
800m north of Torrancroy (GR333165).
(Park 200m north.) A track leads west
towards Rhinstock, reaching a junction
after 600m. Turn right onto a bridge, and

immediately fork left onto a mossy
track which starts to climb through the
plantation. Cross a gravel track to continue
your ascent along the mossy track (50m to
the left). This soon leads out into the open
and up to a bealach between Hill of
Rhinstock and Moss Hill where the track
forks. Turn left to climb west up Moss Hill,
bypassing the summit which has few
distinguishing features. Descend northwards
along the track as it meanders through
peat hags and then suddenly ends, marking
the start of the rougher terrain. Continue
northwest to a cairn before dropping to
cross a track. After climbing the next

knoll, watch for an old path that leads westwards under the broad flanks of Little Geal Charn. It is marked sporadically with cairns, but remains hard to follow in places. When you reach a high point and a track from the south, detour to the summit and back. The path continues westwards, avoiding the vast stretches of peat bog to the north, to reach a bealach and cairn just to the north of Dun Muir. Climb to the summit with its unusual rock marked Mar One. Descend west to enter a world of hags and groughs before following the firmer terrain of the north ridge to the summit and trig point of Carn Mór (GR266184) (3h20). Continue SSW for 1km to the south top.

Descend due east along Monadh an t-Sluich Leith to reach a gravel track which descends to the glen and an intersection by a ruin. Follow the track over the bridge and downstream to another junction after 1km. Continue along the Allt Slochd Chaimbeil: there is a track but it fords the water many times; it is better to keep dry by following the north bank to Duffdefiance. Ford the Littleglen Burn, and follow the track through the plantation and past the Lost Gallery at Aldachuie. After a further 2km, the track reaches two houses by a junction. Turn left rather than taking the road ahead: this leads north to the main road and back to the start (6h20).

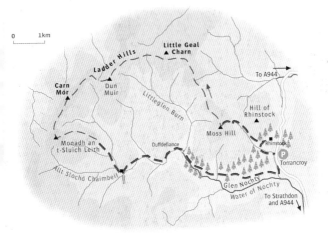

Ben Avon

Ben Avon: Leabaidh an Daimh Bhuidhe
ⓜ (1171m)

Walk time 8h Height gain 900m
Approach and return 2h20 bike or 5h walk
Distance 23km + 22km approach and return
OS Map Landranger 36

A vast plateau broken by tors provides a long and challenging journey. Strath Avon is best accessed by mountain bike.

Start at the parking area for the Queen Victoria viewpoint on the road to Delnabo, 1km south of the eastern end of Tomintoul (GR164176). Follow the dirt track south past the viewpoint to reach a road after 1.5km. Continue up the glen and through a gate at Birchfield: the road turns to gravel before reaching the lodge at Inchrory. Continue 600m south to a bridge over the Builg Burn.

Leave bikes here: walk times start from this point. Cross the bridge, and after 300m turn left to climb southwards by a smaller track. When this fades into the heather, continue to climb southwest. Higher up, a path leads around the north side of Meall Gaineimh to a bealach with two buttresses. From here, the path keeps to the east side of the ridge before disappearing close to East Meur Gorm Craig. Bear southwestwards over folding terrain, keeping to the high ground to reach the top of Mullach Lochan nan Gabhar. The main plateau of Ben Avon forms an interesting horseshoe dotted with useful crags. Continue southwest past a three-tiered buttress, (as seen from the west), then a rectangular block with a diamond-shaped indent, to reach the high crags of Leabaidh an Daimh Bhuidhe, the

summit of Ben Avon (GR132018) (3h40).
Return 1km to where you gained the
plateau, and continue SSE past the castle-
like crag of Clach Choutsaich to the
broken boulders of Stùc Gharbh Mhór
which marks the end of the ridge.
Descend south on steepening slopes
to reach a stalkers' path by the
Allt an Eas Mhóir. This takes
you to the wide strath of the
River Gairn where an
excellent path runs on the
north side for 4.5km and
then leads past moraines
and ruins to a track.
Follow this north,
forking left to pass two
lochans. Take the path
which runs along the
east side of Loch
Builg. Cross the burn
and descend by a
good track to ford the
Builg Burn (or cross by
a footbridge, 300m
south). Continue north to
Inchrory Lodge (8h). Pedal or
walk back to the start.

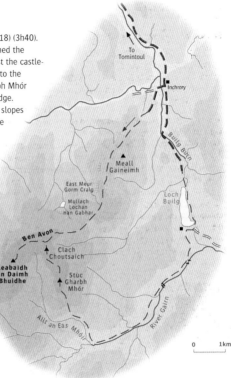

Cairngorm minerals

Within the veins and cavities of the Cairngorm granite is a smoky quartz mineral which
found great popularity with Victorian Scots. A specimen weighing 22kg was discoverd in
1788 near the top of Ben Avon, but it was the late 19th-century fashion for jewel-encrusted
silverware that inspired speculators to spend months in extremely harsh conditions
searching the hillsides for 'Cairngorm' gemstones.

◀ The River Avon near Tomintoul

The Distillery Tour

Carn Daimh (550m)

Walk time 4h **Height gain** 300m
Distance 13km **OS Map** Landranger 36

**An intricate and varied walk by
waymarked paths which lead over
rolling heather hills.**

Start from the parking area at Clash
Wood, just northwest of Tomnavoulin
(GR207264). Pass through the gate to take
a track into the wood. Watch for a turning
on the left after 100m marked as Glenlivet
Estate Route 5. This leaves the forest and
continues above a fenced field, crossing a
stile to reach several farm tracks. Follow the
track directly ahead, which leads southwest

along the glen to Westertown Farm. The
route fords the burn at the farm, climbs in
a zigzag and cuts through a small wood
before rising over a field. A gate takes you
into the forest where the track can be fairly
muddy. At an intersection, turn right to
follow the Speyside Way northwards. After
an initial climb, this drops down and exits
the trees, leaving a final short climb to the
summit of Carn Daimh (GR182251) (2h).
Descend north from the top: the plantation
re-emerges on the west side. [Escape: take a
signposted path east to Tomnavoulin.]
Continue alongside the trees at the end of a
fence at the end of the plantation. An
opening gives access to a good track: take

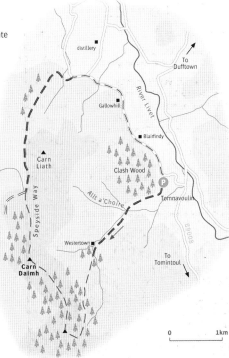

his north to circumnavigate
Carn Liath. The Speyside
Way then descends by a
new plantation, passing a
ruined farmhouse before
coming to the road. Turn
right and walk east for
600m to a junction.
[Detour: turn left for a
quick dram at the
Glenlivet Distillery.]
Turn right again, and
continue southeast
past Gallowhill and
Blairfindy to the
start (4h).

The Glenlivet distillery

A government survey in 1823, which found 14,000 illegal distilleries, resulted in new laws
being proposed by the Duke of Gordon to suppress the stills. Licenses to distil had to be
applied for, and one of the first granted was to the founder of the Glenlivet distillery George
Smith, a latin scholar whose illegal output had reputedly been the favourite of King George
IV. He soon faced competition, however, from many other distilleries that produced whisky
labelled Glen Livet. Following a famous legal battle in 1880 it was ruled that only one could
claim to be 'The Glenlivet'. It is now the biggest selling malt in the US.

◄ Glen Livet above Tomnavoulin

Index

🅜 **Munros** are mountains in Scotland above 914m (3000ft). (Named after Sir Hugh Munro who compiled the first list in 1891.)

🅒 **Corbetts** are peaks between 762m and 914m (2500ft and 3000ft) which have a drop of at least 152m (500ft) on all sides. (Named after John Corbett who drew up the list and made the first ascent.)